Creative Bloom

Projects and Inspiration with Fabric and Wire

Jennifer Swift

NORTH LIGHT BOOKS

Cincinnati, Ohio

14 13 12 11 10   5 4 3 2 1

DISTRIBUTED IN CANADA BY FRASER DIRECT
100 Armstrong Avenue
Georgetown, ON, Canada L7G 5S4
Tel: (905) 877-4411

DISTRIBUTED IN THE U.K. AND EUROPE BY
F+W INTERNATIONAL
Brunel House, Newton Abbot, Devon, TQ12 4PU, England
Tel: (+44) 1626 323200, Fax: (+44) 1626 323319
E-mail: postmaster@davidandcharles.co.uk

DISTRIBUTED IN AUSTRALIA BY CAPRICORN LINK
P.O. Box 704, S. Windsor NSW, 2756 Australia
Tel: (02) 4577-3555

Library of Congress Cataloging in Publication Data
Swift, Jennifer
  Creative bloom : projects and inspiration with fabric and wire / Jennifer Swift. -- 1st ed.
     p. cm.
  Includes index.
  ISBN-13: 978-1-4403-0316-6 (pbk. : alk. paper)
  1. Fabric flowers. 2. Wire craft. I. Title.
  TT890.5.S95 2010
  745.56--dc22

                    2010013735

Metric Conversion Chart

TO CONVERT	TO	MULTIPLY BY
Inches	Centimeters	2.54
Centimeters	Inches	0.4
Feet	Centimeters	30.5
Centimeters	Feet	0.03
Yards	Meters	0.9
Meters	Yards	1.1

fw media
www.fwmedia.com

Editor: Rachel Scheller

Designer: Geoff Raker

Production Coordinator: Greg Nock

Photographer: Ric Deliantoni

Stylist: Nora Martini

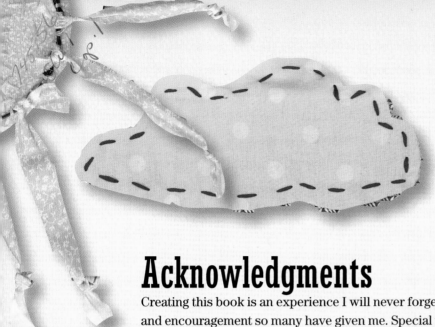

Dedication

To Jeremy, my MacGyver, who always manages to ground my flights of fancy and make them a reality. Thank you for giving so much of your time to make this book happen. I love you. To my parents for supporting both my art and my dreams; without your love and care I wouldn't be who I am. To my little boy, who let his mommy be an artist for a while. Yes, sweetie, *now* we can go play!

Acknowledgments

Creating this book is an experience I will never forget. I am overwhelmed by the generous support and encouragement so many have given me. Special thanks to Tonia and to my editor, Rachel. I am extremely grateful to both of you for your guidance throughout this process. This book is better than I could ever have hoped because you, Christine, Geoff and the North Light staff all contributed your talents and time to make it so. Thanks to my friends and family who encouraged me, especially Becky, Kristen, Shelley, Lori and Audrey, who were my companions throughout this book's creation. I'd also like to thank Monica for opening up her home and her schedule to my son and giving me the gift of uninterrupted time. I also feel a debt of gratitude to all the artist teachers out there who have shared their work and ideas so generously with the rest of us. Special thanks to two artists, Shelley and Teri, for sharing their work with me. One final acknowledgment to God for giving me this task and the ability to complete it. I am so grateful.

About the Author

Jennifer Swift is a mixed-media artist living in the Minneapolis, Minnesota area with her sweetheart of a husband and adorable little son. Jen always wanted to be an artist when she grew up . . . and a doctor, and a poet, and a fashion designer, architect and cheerleader. The daughter of two teachers, she spent much of her time at school. To pass the time she would spend hours drawing cloud cities (inspired by *Star Wars*) on her mother's chalkboard. She enjoyed making clothes for her dolls out of tissue and also read incessantly.

Once she grew up, Jen embarked on a career as a floral designer. For several years she divided her time between floral design and a volunteer position teaching art to children. She met and married her husband, and when their son was born she became a stay-at-home mom. Needing a creative outlet, she began to create little wire flower gardens. At the same time, she also began to play around with fabric for the first time. Inspired, she combined the wire and fabric and soon opened her own Etsy shop, Bird From a Wire, to sell her work. Jen also took the chance to submit her work to several national art publications and was elated to have her work included in such magazines as *Sew Somerset* and *Somerset Home*. She has since been living the life of an artist, her childhood dream come true. This book is another dream come true for Jen. She loves to create and loves to inspire others to create as well, and this book allows her to do both.

Jen recently embarked on a creative quest to shape all things metal to her will and is excited to share this and her other artistic (mis)adventures with you through her blog, http://blog.birdfromawire.com.

Table of Contents

Resolutions for My

Creative growth

This Year I will....

Fill a sketchbook page a day
with ideas or doodles.

Blog 4-5 times every week!

Make time daily to play!

Do one thing every day to promote my work.

Follow one new path everyday.

Encourage someone daily!!!

Introduction

Within each of us grows a garden. When we are young, it grows wild. It blooms without any help or care from us. The flowers of this garden are the ideas and inspirations of our child artist; they are beautiful and grow abundantly. The soil in which they grow is made of our dreams. As we grow, we pick these flowers without thought for the future. Then comes a season when the flowers that once grew wild cease to grow and bloom.

Gardens, you see, need care if they are to continue to grow. The soil needs to be cultivated, and the seeds of inspiration need to be sown. When fresh new shoots of thoughts and ideas sprout, we need to tend them carefully. Very few of us know this instinctively. We learn through trial and error how best to garden our plots. We search out other gardener artists, learn their methods, and, when we can, apply them to our own gardens. Books are a wonderful way to share this knowledge.

The philosophy of this book is simple. It follows the principle that if you give an artist a flower, she's happy for a day. Teach her to grow her own, and she's happy for a lifetime. The projects I've chosen to fill these pages will teach you wire-bending and fabric techniques you'll be able to use again and again. The chapters will encourage you to see the seeds of inspiration in the world around you: in your home, your closet, your family and friends—even the view outside your window. You'll be encouraged to identify and develop your personal imagery and style so you can use the techniques to create art that is uniquely yours.

Along the way, I'll share with you the story of my garden, including the tools, planting methods and design ideas I've discovered or developed. Your garden is unique. The soil, the growing conditions and the challenges each artist experiences are personal and depend on the individual. What you decide to plant, how you choose to fertilize or encourage growth and your design focus will all be unique to you. There will never be another garden just like yours.

It is my hope that this book will help you cultivate your garden. That you'll feel inspired to clear the ground and dig in. That you will see your garden thrive and bloom, and that others will see in our gardens the possibilities for their own. I imagine a world filled with people who have gardens of inspiration growing and blooming within them, a world of people enjoying their own *Creative Bloom*.

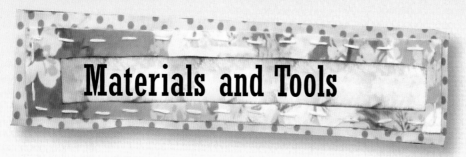

Materials and Tools

The projects in this book require several materials and tools. Some you may be familiar with; others may be entirely new. Below I've listed the most common ones to get you started.

Wire

Wire comes in a variety of gauges. The gauge of a wire refers to its thickness. The higher the gauge, the thinner the wire. For example, a 16-gauge wire is thicker than a 19-gauge wire.

Sixteen-gauge dark annealed steel wire can be purchased at your local hardware store and can usually be located with the rebar. This wire is coated in oil and must be wiped off with a rag or paper towel as you use it. It is often referred to as tie wire or baling wire.

Nineteen-gauge dark annealed steel wire is also referred to as craft wire and can be purchased at most craft stores. This wire is combined with the 16-gauge wire in many of the projects in this book.

Copper wire can be found in a variety of gauges in most craft, art or jewelry supply stores.

Fabric

The majority of the fabrics used in this book are found in the quilting fabrics section of your local fabric store. Not only do these fabrics come in a fabulous selection of colors and patterns, but they also seem to be the perfect weight to combine with wire. Although it's recommended by the manufacturer that you wash these fabrics before use to remove the starch in them, I find the extra starch helpful when stitching fabric to wire.

All the projects in this book use fabric. Some call specifically for fabric scraps, fabric pieces or strips of fabric. Many of the projects were initially created to make use of those bits of fabric scraps that are often too small to be saved. For the purposes of completing a project, a scrap refers to a piece of fabric that is larger than 3"–4" (8cm–10cm) but smaller than ¼ yard (23cm). A fabric strip is between ½" (1.5cm) and 1" (2.5cm) wide and varies in length. Strips are typically tied onto wire as accents.

Sewing Notions

Iron-on fusible interfacing is a product used in this book to add weight or strength to fabric.

Quilt batting and stuffing comes in polyester, cotton or bamboo fill. I love the Warm & Natural cotton quilt batting and like the touch of the bamboo stuffing best.

Embroidery floss comes in practically any color imaginable. The colors you use in each project are personal design choices and are left up to you. However, I consider DMC #844 the best match for the dark annealed wire used in many of the book's projects.

Pliers

Needle-nose pliers come in either short- or long-nose versions. Dig around your toolbox and you'll most likely discover you already own these pliers. These are fine to begin with, but the larger handles will cause fatigue if you use them often. Purchasing a jewelry-tool version of these pliers from a craft or jewelry supply store is inexpensive and really makes a difference in how you experience this craft. After several years of using my inexpensive jewelry pliers, I recently upgraded to Lindstrom Rx pliers because of their ergonomic benefits. I absolutely love them!

Flat-nose pliers are optional but are very handy for clamping or flattening cut ends of wire.

Round-nose pliers are used in the jewelry section of this book to create loops of wire. If you have an interest in beginning jewelry making, these are a must-have tool.

Cutters

Heavy-duty wire cutters are found in the electrical supply area of any hardware store. This tool works best for cutting 16-gauge annealed steel wire. If you use your jewelry wire cutters with this wire, they will dull quickly, so reserve them for thinner-gauged wire only.

Flush cutters are used to create a straight, flush cut in wire. They are listed as an optional tool in the jewelry section of this book, where they are used to cut wire coils to create jump rings.

Needles

Sewing needles are purchased in packs and come in different types and sizes. The type of needle you choose is usually based on the size or type of thread you are stitching with and the type of fabric you are stitching into. As a personal preference, I like to use chenille needles in size 18 when working with embroidery floss because they have a larger head, making threading easier. When beading, a smaller size of beading needle is usually necessary.

Needle threaders are optional but are an inexpensive purchase that may really increase your enjoyment of this craft. They are usually located near the needles in a quilt or craft store.

Scissors

Small, sharp scissors make detailed cutting into and around fabric shapes easy. Although there are a variety of embroidery scissors that will work, I prefer the inexpensive version made by IKEA. They seem to be the perfect size for trim work and are more comfortable to use.

Fabric scissors are best for cutting longer lengths of fabric. Be sure to reserve these scissors for cutting fabric only. Using them to cut paper will dull them and ruin them for fabric work.

Mandrel

A mandrel is a tool, usually a rod of some sort, around which wire can be wrapped. A mandrel could be a dowel rod, a knitting needle, a pen barrel or anything else you might find to serve your purpose. I frequently use the metal rod from my floor sweeper, as it is the right diameter for many of the projects and the wire slides easily off the metal.

Some of the projects in this book will suggest you wrap the wire around an object, such as a wine bottle, to form a specific shape. You might choose to use a different object to vary the size and shape of your finished wire form.

Mixed-Media Tools and Materials

Water-soluble crayons, Inktense pencils, fabric markers and paint markers are a few mark-making products you might like to try. Shiva's Paintstiks are also worth experimenting with, as they create lovely, color-rich marks on fabric.

Acrylic paints are divided into two categories: artist-grade paints sold in tubes, and craft paints usually sold in bottles. The type you choose depends on your project. I keep a selection of both. I also love using Ranger's Distress Crackle Paint because of the wonderful texture it creates.

In this book, we'll be using ink pads when stamping or tinting fabric. Two of my favorites are the Archival brand (which works great with photo-quality stamps) and Ranger's Distress Inks.

In several projects, we'll also be making embellishments with polymer clay. I prefer Studio by Sculpey because it is easy to condition and form and comes in a beautiful assortment of colors. Any polymer clay may be substituted, but carefully read and follow the manufacturer's instructions and recommendations for safe use.

Spray Paint

I've had good luck with Rust-Oleum spray paint, which is found in most hardware stores. Its American Accents line now comes in a large assortment of "fashion" colors, although I'm still partial to the lovely rust color of its base primer. Remember to use spray paint in a well-ventilated area and to follow the manufacturer's instructions.

Craft Sheet

Several of the projects in this book suggest you paint, ink, glue or otherwise make a mess on your work surface. Using a craft sheet as your palette or as a surface to work on makes cleanup a breeze. Paint, glue, acrylic mediums and resin all scrape right off once dried. Ink wipes off cleanly. The craft sheet is also the ideal nonstick surface for creating fabric pages, such as those found in the *Upcycled Art Journal* (see page 40).

CHAPTER 1

Clearing the Soil

Beginning the Process of Renewal

Gardens are always growing. If tended and planted, they produce beautiful blooms, but if left to fend for themselves, weeds will soon take over. In the corner of my yard is a large garden plot that has been there since we purchased our house. The first spring we were in our home, I went crazy and planted several varieties of tomatoes, herbs, lettuce, cucumbers and peppers. I used a specially prepared fertilizer and watered diligently. As you may have guessed, my crop that year was huge. The next year, I planted everything just as I had the year before. I tended the garden, weeded and watered, and just as everything was starting to take off . . . I left on vacation for two weeks. While the garden had looked great when I left, when I returned everything was wilted, the tomato plants were spindly and nothing was growing well but the weeds, which were everywhere. I tried to remedy the situation, but, deprived of a healthy start, the garden never did recover.

Over the next few years, I tried again and again to mimic my first year's efforts but was unsuccessful each time. Discouraged, I eventually left the garden alone, and the weeds completely overtook it.

Since then I've gathered information and done a little research that has given me a sense of what went wrong. First and foremost, don't leave for vacation just as your plants are starting to take root and grow! Depriving them of regular watering at this stage is pretty much the worst thing you can do. Second, don't plant the same crops in the same spots year after year. It turns out there are

nutrients in the soil the plants use up as they grow—who knew? If your plants consume all the nutrients during one season, there won't be any left for the next. The third thing I learned is that weeds have long been the champions of the garden's "Survival of the Fittest" contest. If you allow weeds to live in the same area as your plants, they will grow, and your plants will not.

So what does all this have to do with being an artist? Through experience, I've found that the process of planting and tending a garden is much like the process of living an inspired life. In order to reach that "blooming time" we all desire, we must dig deep within ourselves, turn over the soil and sow some seeds. We must play the role of garden designers and experiment with new techniques and mediums so we can discover ways to amend and fertilize our creative soil. It does take time and work; however, if you've ever tried to clear a garden of weeds and ready it for planting, you know it doesn't really take finesse—all you really need is some time and a dedication to starting fresh.

I've learned a lot of things through experience, but I've also been lucky enough to find individuals with experience who have generously shared their knowledge with me. I'm very grateful to them, and this book is my opportunity to do the same. I'd like to share with you my experiences growing and developing my artist life. I believe many of you will see yourselves in this story and find some tips or encouragement to help you grow and develop your artistic nature.

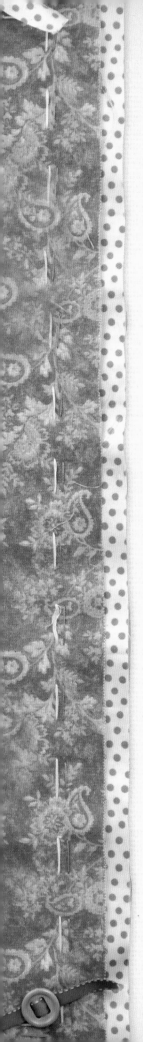

The Beginning

My story began over thirteen years ago in a garden. Actually, it was just a mound of still-frozen dirt outside my college's studio-arts building. In another month it would be planted, but at this time of year it was looking a little barren. Upon seeing the plot, it occurred to me that the next day was March 21, the official first day of spring. However, I was in a northern climate, and there was still snow on the ground. It didn't feel anything like spring at the time, and there was nothing yet that even hinted of change.

That night, thinking of that sad little bare patch, I picked up some wire and bent them into flowers. I scavenged some sticks from outside and wrapped my wire around them to form stems. I wove waxed linen thread through the wire petals to add color. When I was finished, I went outside and planted my little flowers in the empty garden plot. On the sidewalk around it, in chalk, I wrote *Celebrate March 21, the first day of spring!*

The next morning when I arrived for class, I discovered that the entire building was talking and wondering about my little sculpture garden. The surprise seemed to have turned the day into something special for a lot of people. It was the first time I witnessed my art making a difference in the lives of others. It was also the first time I sculpted my little wire flowers. I didn't make another one for thirteen years, but I did keep one just to remind me of the experience. I had no idea that years later it would inspire me again.

After school, I decided to try my hand at floral design. I loved flowers, and the act of creating with them suited me. My dream was to be an artist, but I couldn't seem to figure out how to actually become one. I decided to make do with the career at hand, yet I wasn't completely satisfied. I was living an artful life but wanted, in my heart of hearts, an art-filled one.

Over the years, I tried to start my art again, but I would become frustrated right away by a lack of inspiration. What had come easily in college just wasn't there now. I tried drawing from my life as it was, but I didn't know how to find inspiration in baby bottles or my suburban surroundings. I wasn't inspired by my life as it was and knew I wouldn't be able to find inspiration anywhere else. This scared me, and I gave up temporarily.

But dreams don't like to wait, and mine tugged at me until one day I had an epiphany. I realized I could still create art without being fueled by inspiration or emotion. Art could be playful and could be created just to experience the joy of creating. I decided to stop waiting and start working. I wanted to give myself the chance to play without feeling critical about what I created, so I decided against renewing my painting or drawing pursuits. Instead, I picked up wire and fabric.

Once I made the choice to simply begin, the inspiration came. It flowed from the fabric and the wire. It prompted me to combine the two and create something unique. I began to develop my vague thoughts and imaginings in a sketchbook, and I created an inspiration board. I decided to make Wednesday nights my art nights and to create without the expectation of producing anything "good." I allowed myself to enjoy art again.

That was the beginning for me. The small commitment to just "make stuff" once a week is what led me to where I am now. In the process, I had learned how I could live the artist's life I had always wanted to live.

In the following chapter, I'll introduce you to the tools and methods I use to encourage the growth of ideas and

"I learned . . . that inspiration does not come like a bolt, nor is it kinetic, energetic striving, but it comes into us slowly and quietly and all the time, though we must regularly and every day give it a little chance to start flowing, prime it with a little solitude and idleness."

— BRENDA UELAND

Prepare for Planting

With a piece of paper and a pen, take some time to write an assessment of the current state of your garden. What will it take to clear it out and prepare it again for planting? Do a little digging and turn over your dreams. Remove any rocks life may have tossed in your way. Remember the garden of your childhood and then envision this garden renewed. What plans do you have for it? What would you like to grow?

inspiration in my life, as well as the techniques I use to develop those ideas into works of wire and fabric.

If you're having trouble finding inspiration, or the ideas just don't come as quickly as they once did, don't despair. Inspiration will bloom for you as it has for me. Be ready to recognize it because it will come in all sorts of ways and sizes.

It will be in the vision you glimpse that inspires you to begin a new work. It will be the crazy thought you can't seem to get out of your head and the daring impulse that pushes you to try something new. It will be there as you tend your garden and encourage its growth. You, too, will be living an art-filled life.

Blooming Flower Key Chain

Flowers are pretty to look at, but for me they also symbolize the need to stop and be aware of the moment. A flower's blooming period is just a brief part of its life cycle. It is the beauty of this blooming time, though, that causes us to stop and notice what we otherwise would have passed by.

When I started to play with wire, I created flowers to surround me and remind me to slow down. Making these flowers would be a great place for you to begin as well. They're very simply executed and take just a little practice. This fabric and wire key chain is an introductory project that will acquaint you with some basic wire-bending and fabric-stitching techniques.

MATERIALS

anti-fray medium

1"–2" (2.5cm–5cm) chain (optional)

16-gauge dark annealed steel wire

embroidery floss

fabric scraps

6mm jump ring (optional)

key ring

rag or paper towel

TOOLS

needle-nose pliers

scissors

sewing needle

small paintbrush

wire cutters

TECHNIQUES

Bending Wire

Stitching Fabric to Wire

Thoughts While Creating

As with sketching, when you work with wire you'll find yourself sometimes using your whole arm. The wire has a definite tension to it, and working with the tension will help your sculptures look intuitive, as if they are naturally flowing into the form you are shaping.

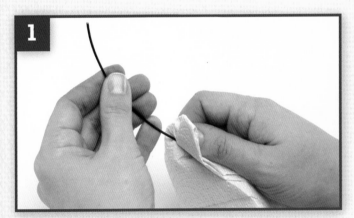

Pull an arm's length of wire from the spool, straightening and wiping the wire with a rag or paper towel as you pull.

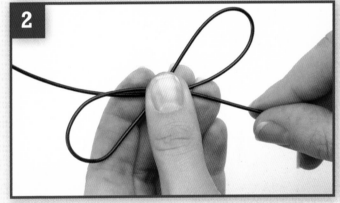

Make a 1" (2.5cm) loop about 1" (2.5cm) from the cut end of the wire. Pulling from the spool, make another 1" (2.5cm) loop opposite the first. You should be holding a figure-eight shape. Wrap the cut end of the wire tightly around the center of the figure-eight to secure.

Tip

Place the spool on the floor and stand as you pull and wipe the wire. This provides the best slack-to-tension ratio for working with the wire, making it easier to sculpt with.

3

Continue as in Step 2 to create 3 more petals, positioning them to create a flower shape. Wrap the wire around the center of the flower after making each petal.

4

Wrap the wire around the center of the flower a few more times, varying the position each time. Wrap the wire loosely across the back to create a loose loop for connecting to a key ring. Wrap the wire around the center once more. Cut the wire from the spool. Use needle-nose pliers to adjust the shape of the petals.

5

Using needle-nose pliers, bend the cut end inward so it doesn't protrude.

6

Using embroidery floss and a needle, stitch a piece of fabric to a wire petal by placing the fabric beneath the petal and bringing the needle up on 1 side of the wire and down on the opposite side. When the petal is stitched, knot the thread and trim any extra floss.

Tip

For a stiffer, more durable fabric, iron the scraps onto fusible interfacing first and then sew them onto the wire petals.

7

Using small scissors, trim the fabric around the petal, leaving a ¼" (6mm) allowance. Repeat Steps 6 and 7 for the remaining petals.

8

Brush the underside of each petal with an anti-fray medium. Be sure to cover the stitching and the edges of the fabric petals. Allow the medium to dry.

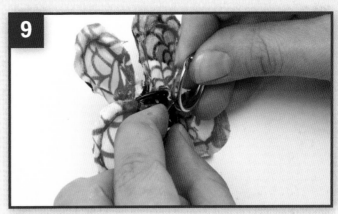

9

Attach a key ring to the loop on the back of the flower. If you want the key chain to dangle more, attach a 1"–2" (2.5cm–5cm) piece of chain to the wire loop with a jump ring. Attach the key ring to the other end of the chain and watch it swing!

Variation

Blooming Flower Sculpture

Wouldn't you love to have one of these blooming flowers on your desk? It's a bit of spring whenever you need it. Instead of cutting the wire when you're finished with the flower head, pull more wire from the spool and straighten it to form the stem. Halfway down the length of your stem, create a figure-eight as demonstrated on page 15, Step 2.

To create the flower's cork base, you'll need an old cork, a metal washer and spray paint. First, spray paint the washer and let it dry. Glue the cork to the washer with craft glue or superglue. Let the glue dry and then push the flower stem at least ¾" (2cm) into the cork. Bend the stem to one side or the other until your sculpture is balanced and stable. Create several of these for an indoor sculpture garden!

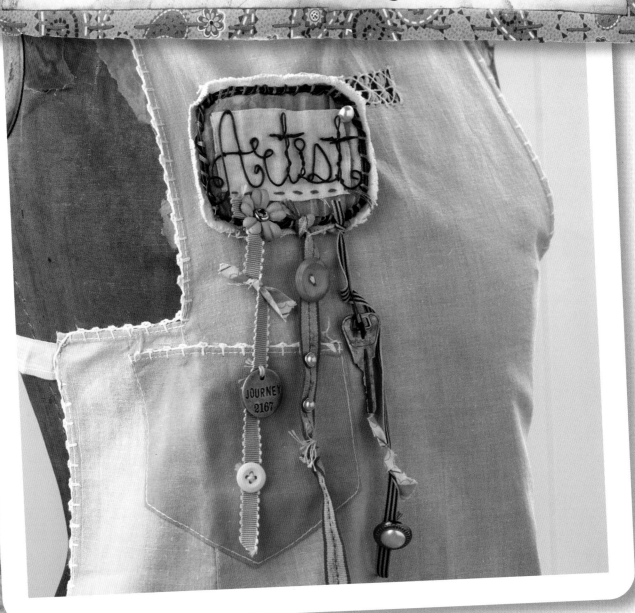

For years I struggled to answer the question "What is your job?" I wanted to say, "I'm an artist!" but it seemed like such a bold claim, especially when I wasn't producing much work and not selling any of it. This made me feel vulnerable, so I'd usually mumble an answer and hope the conversation would move in another direction.

Then one day, while I was attempting to convince a friend she could call herself an artist, I realized I should take my own advice. My friend was visual and surrounded herself with beauty; I saw those same characteristics in myself. She felt happy and energized when creating—so did I.

I realize now that the word *artist* describes who I am and how I think, live and dream. I want to encourage you to see yourself as others probably do and claim the title for yourself. Back up your claim by creating this badge. After completing the basic badge, embellish it by adding colors and objects you love. Make it an original, just like you!

MATERIALS

adhesive pin back

canvas fabric

cardboard

19-gauge craft wire

16-gauge dark
annealed steel wire

embroidery floss

muslin fabric

pencil

piece of paper

spray paint (optional)

Finishing the Project

brads

buttons

found objects

metal
embellishments

ribbons

TOOLS

flat- or needle-nose
pliers

scissors

sewing needle

wire cutters

TECHNIQUES

Forming Words
from Wire

Creating a Frame
Around a Wire Word

Securing Wire
Elements to a
Soft Substrate

Thoughts While Creating

It is often easier to create wire
words by using a written template.
Use the template as a reference as
you form the word in wire.

Write the word artist in cursive with a pencil and paper to create
a written template. (You can also use the template on page 123
as a guide.)

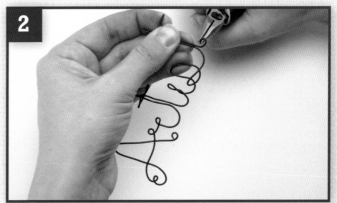

Using 19-gauge wire and flat- or needle-nose pliers, bend
directly on top of your writing or simply look at the template for
reference as you form the word. I usually choose the latter as I
find I achieve a more graceful, flowing effect this way. To prevent
snags or scratches, begin each word by bending the cut end of
the wire in on itself.

"Every child is an artist. The problem is how to remain an artist once we grow up."

— PABLO PICASSO

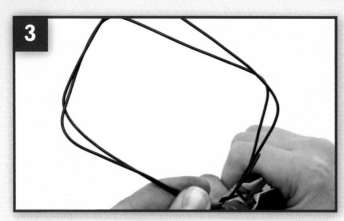

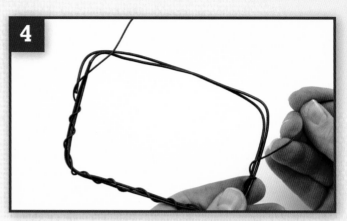

Place the word in front of you and shape a rectangular wire frame to fit loosely around the word with 16-gauge wire. Use your hand to bend the wire for a rounded bend, or use pliers if you'd like a sharper angle. Shape a second layer of wire over the first rectangle and then cut the wire.

Pull 7" (18cm) of 19-gauge wire from the spool. Hold the wire to the frame and begin wrapping both rectangular outlines together. Hold the wire taut and wrap it under and around the frame. When the 7" (18cm) length is wrapped, use the wire from the spool to wrap wire tautly around the rest of the frame.

Tip

At this point, you may choose to spray paint your frame and wire word with the color of your choice. Let the paint dry before continuing.

Cut a piece of muslin that is slightly longer than the wire frame, but not wider. Cut pieces of cardboard and canvas that are longer and wider than the wire frame. Layer the muslin over the cardboard and place the canvas at the bottom of the stack. Place the wire frame on top of the stack. With embroidery floss and a needle, stitch the fabric stack to the wire frame.

6

Using scissors designated for paper, trim the cardboard closely around the frame. Using fabric scissors, trim the fabric around the frame as well. Leave at least a ¼" (6mm) minimum allowance around the frame.

7

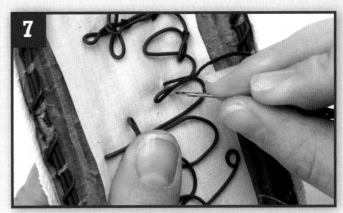

Place the wire word in the center of the badge and stitch it into place with embroidery floss, sewing through all the layers. Place stitches at the beginning and end of the word and at the top and bottom of each letter. More stitches may be needed to secure the word adequately. Position an adhesive pin back on the back of the badge and press it into place.

Finishing the Project

To add movement and flair, try tying or stitching ribbons to the bottom of your badge. I chose three ribbons of varying lengths and tied them to the wire frame of my badge. Rummage through your collection of odds and ends and pull out an assortment of smaller items you would like to include. I chose a small key that says *Do Not Duplicate*, a Tim Holtz ideology pendant and some assorted buttons and brads. The brads were inserted right through the ribbon; the rest were stitched on with embroidery floss.

"DRAW EVERYWHERE AND ALL THE TIME. AN ARTIST IS A SKETCHBOOK WITH A PERSON ATTACHED."

— IRWIN GREENBERG

CHAPTER 2

The Tool Shed

Gathering What You Need

Any good gardener or artist knows that possessing the right tools for a job is very important. Working without tools often leads to frustration and a botched job. Good tools will aid you and allow you to create at a higher level than you would have been able to attain without them. Although there are many development tools available to the artist, I want to discuss three of the most basic: the sketchbook, the inspiration board and the journal. I've found these tools to be invaluable. You may already be familiar with them, and you might already own and use them on a regular basis. Some of you may choose to combine your sketchbook and journal, and that is just fine, but for clarity, I'll refer to them separately. Throughout this book, I will be encouraging you to use these tools for specific exercises, so I recommend that you supply yourself with them before you begin.

The Sketchbook

The first tool is the sketchbook. This is a blank book you will use regularly to record and develop your visual ideas. I think of mine as a "catchall" to record my ideas and flashes of inspiration so I will remember them later. Almost every night I wake up at three or four o'clock in the morning and lie with my eyes closed, just thinking. I've found that this space of time between waking and sleeping is one of my most imaginative and inspiring. I lie in my bed fresh from a dream state and begin to think. I mull over problems, picture ideas and images, and make connections that are unattainable to my conscious, busy, daytime mind. Then I get up, locate my sketchbook and sneak into the kitchen to quickly sketch out ideas and images or jot down answers to questions I have. Only then can I go back to sleep.

You might not be experiencing this midnight sojourn now, but you will. When you begin to cultivate inspiration, you're giving inspiration an open door and asking it to come whenever it can. It often seems to choose a time that's horribly inconvenient, like when you're driving the car or grocery shopping. For me, it rarely comes when I'm sitting down and purposefully trying to develop an idea. Having a sketchbook handy allows you to collect these quick visions and answers as they come to you. So carry it around with you. Keep it in your purse; bring it with you regardless of your activity. It'll soon feel like a part of you. A reporter is never without his notebook, and artists should never be without their sketchbooks. If you can't fit the one you have into your purse or coat pocket, buy a second smaller one. I've had many sketchbooks through the years, and I can still open any one of them and glean a fresh thought or idea to develop.

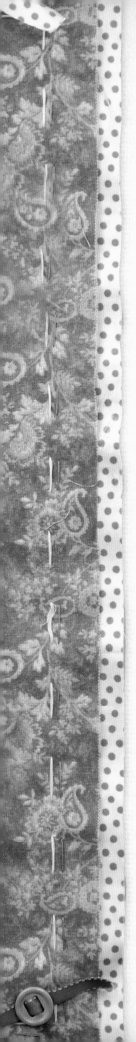

The Inspiration Board

The second tool is the inspiration board. This is a big corkboard you'll hang on a wall somewhere prominent so you can see it regularly. Don't put it in the unused corner of your basement—this needs to be front and center! I keep mine in my art room directly across from the hallway door. Then I can glance at it whenever I'm walking by. The images I've posted stay fresh in my mind this way, and because of this, my mind continues to develop them as I do other things. The board is another tried-and-true tool for cultivating inspiration. Sometimes referred to as a vision board or collage board, I think of it as a place to put my "lovelies": little bits of photos or drawings I love to meditate on. Our artist selves like to save all kinds of things, just because we like them. It might be a bit of napkin that has a spaghetti smear in the shape of the Mona Lisa, or maybe paint chips in a color combination you just love. It could be a postcard of someone else's art, or a leaf you picked up on your daily walk. The inspiration board is the place to put them all. The board fills up fast, and you'll start to pin new items over the old. This works as a culling process, allowing you to identify the images you feel are the most important. You'll also find it's a great tool for making unexpected connections. Glancing from the chartreuse and purple color swatch to the photo of a necklace torn from a magazine might inspire you to combine the two in a way that might not have occurred to you otherwise.

The Journal

The third tool I couldn't do without is the journal. This is the place to write the thoughts that sometimes clutter your mind. It's also the perfect place to explore and develop the little "flits" of inspiration that need a place to land. As you write, you can develop these "flits" and give them substance. You can also use your journal to take notes on the processes and projects you are exploring throughout the course of this book. I want to emphasize that this is the place to write; however, if you need to draw a sketch of how you feel to release the words, go ahead.

Both writing journals and art journals can exist in the artist's toolbox. I've used both. In chapter 3, there is an example of an art journal I created from one journal entry (see pages 40–43). What I wrote initially in my journal became the basis of a wonderful work that is an inspirational journal of both words and pictures.

Other Useful Tools

An optional tool I'd recommend as well is a camera. As visual artists, sometimes we see things while we're out and about that inspire a new series of work in the studio. Keeping a camera with you allows you to take a visual note you can return to later. When you arrive home, you can then print these pictures and tape them into your sketchbook with notes about what you thought or felt. If the unusual color of the sky on a particular night strikes you, write it down. If seeing the silhouette of a lone bird at the very top of a tree makes you wonder briefly what it sees, write it down. Also, although you may think you'll remember why you took a picture of something, I find it's a good idea to jot down some notes, too. Life has a way of speeding by, and these quick visions and inspirations are easily lost when you start to focus on your grocery list and errands instead.

These tools will help you do the work of cultivating inspiration. It is work, though, and approaching it with a sense of commitment is extremely important. To

Cultivating Inspiration

A Trip to the Museum

With your journal in hand, take a walk through your local museum or gallery. Walk quickly to gather quick impressions of the art. Mark in your mind which works you instantly feel drawn to and those you instantly dislike. Then turn around and walk back through, pausing in front of the pieces you liked. Draw a quick sketch of each piece. Scribble a brief description of what attracts you. Then turn around again and do the same for the pieces you didn't like. Ask yourself what repelled you. Was it the colors? The composition? The subject matter? A professor once told me that discovering our dislikes is often more revealing of our artistic personality than finding things we love. Pause to think about what your collection of ideas and impressions could be revealing about you. Then, before you leave, be sure to stop by the museum shop and pick up a few postcards of the works you wrote about. When you get home, paste them into your sketchbook as a visual reminder of your trip. Next to each card, jot down why you chose each one. Pin your favorite one to your inspiration board. Keeping a sketchbook of your thoughts on works of art and your art experiences will, over time, provide you with a fabulous collection to inspire you. Pinning your favorite image to your inspiration board keeps the image fresh. By using both tools, you've planned for inspiration now and later.

be the creative, productive artist you want to be will take some time. If you learn to cultivate yourself and your surroundings gainfully, you will never ever be at a loss. You'll be able to reference your sketch-book, inspiration board or journal and find the inspiration to carry you on. These are tools you can use all your life, and I promise that if you do, you'll find you have a lifetime's worth of ideas to work with.

Sketchbooks may be utilitarian tools for artists, but I still like mine to be pretty. It's much more fun to pull out my sketchbook if it's colorful, has dangling charms and fabric strips, and looks like a work of art. I've always decorated my covers, and now, when I pull an old one off the shelf, it sparks my memory to see the images or art from that time period.

When I created my sketchbook I was working with a fabric-and-wire combination and chose copper as my metal. Copper is softer than steel and is easy to flatten and use as an embellishment.

I encourage you to give these techniques a try. You might decide to make yours as shown, or you may choose to create your own design. Just make sure your cover is one you'll love to show off, use and carry with you everywhere!

MATERIALS

16-gauge copper wire
collage paper
E-6000 glue
fabric scraps
glue stick
hardcover, spiral-bound sketchbook with plain black cover

Finishing the Project
buttons
6" × 8" (15cm × 20.5cm) fabric piece
fabric strips
pencil or pen
rub-on letters

TOOLS

needle- or round-nose pliers
scissors
small hammer with flat head
steel block
wire cutters
wooden craft stick

TECHNIQUES

Creating Wire-Flower Embellishments
Flattening Copper Wire

Notes on the Process

Don't feel as though you need a complete vision of a work before you start it. Allowing some details to remain uncertain leaves room for spontaneous inspirations that come as you are creating. In the end, those are often the brightest spots.

This project definitely developed in a collage manner. I knew I wanted to include hammered copper, but the rest of the design was a question. The full design came to me once I had begun working on it, giving me the sense that I was interacting with the art as it was created. It was rather like a conversation: "She said _____, so I said_____." Much of the composition wouldn't have come to me if I'd started with a full sketch that mapped out every detail.

Collage the surface of the sketchbook by layering scraps of fabric or paper with a glue stick. Feel free to doodle or add decorative stitching to your background as well.

To create a spiral flower, grip the end of the copper wire with needle- or round-nose pliers. Working from the spool, bend the wire into a spiral shape that extends from the cut end. The spiral can be tight or loose—it's up to you. Once the spiral is the desired size, bend the wire away from it at a ninety-degree angle.

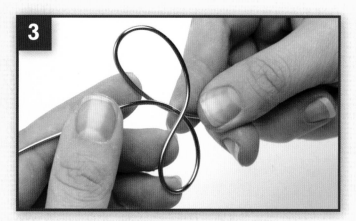

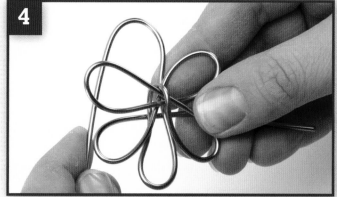

Without cutting the wire, create a figure-eight approximately 2"–3" (5cm–7.5cm) down from the spiral flower head. These are the flower's leaves. Wrap the wire once around the center of the figure-eight, and then continue to straighten the next 2"–4" (5cm–10cm) of wire to form the rest of the flower stem. Cut the wire from the spool.

Create a daisy shape, using the same technique as for the *Blooming Flower Key Chain* (see pages 16 and 17, Steps 2–5). However, after forming the first 5 petals, add more petals as desired. Unlike with the flower key chain, wrap the wire around the center sparingly. Make 2 copper flowers, 1 larger than the other.

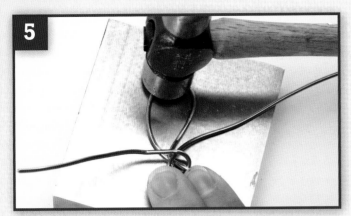

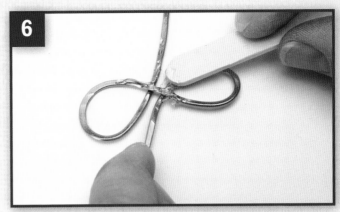

Using a small hammer and a steel block, gently tap the wire flowers flat. The thinner you pound the wire, the more likely it is to break, so don't pound the wire too flat. Place the flowers on the sketchbook cover to ensure they will lay flat against the surface. Make adjustments with the hammer and steel block if necessary. The entire surface of the wire must lie flat on the cover to ensure a strong bond when it is glued.

Use a wooden craft stick to spread a thin layer of E-6000 glue on the back of a wire flower. Flip the flower over and place it on the sketchbook cover. Adhere the remaining flowers in the same way. Place a heavy object on top of the wire flowers to ensure a strong bond.

Finishing the Project

Using E-6000 glue or superglue, adhere a button to each flower's center. Add any other flower accents as desired. Cut a butterfly image from a 6" × 8" (15cm × 20.5cm) piece of fabric and adhere it to the upper left corner of the cover with a glue stick. (I used Floragraphix II by Jason Yenter from In the Beginning Fabrics.) Use rub-on letters to spell out the words *sketch* and *book* in the center of your composition. Using a pencil or pen, draw the butterfly's flight path around the title. Cut fabric strips and tie them to the wire binding. Add the date if you desire, and enjoy your sketchbook!

29

Inspiration Board

I discovered the concept for the inspiration board by accident. Someone had given me a corkboard, and because I was short on floor and table space in my apartment, I hung it up. Over the next few months I began to see the value of this space, as various visual inspirations were pinned to the board and viewed every day.

It occurred to me recently to make my inspiration board truly inspirational. I could treat it as a frame or a canvas that was both unique and fit for display. It wasn't long after this that I found a very inexpensive, dilapidated corkboard at a local rummage sale. By adding a little wire and fabric, it was transformed from old rummage into a rather inspired inspiration board.

In this project, I'll demonstrate some of the techniques I used to transform my board, such as carving a stamp, printing on cork and adding other decorative, personal touches. Grab your board and materials, and let's get started!

MATERIALS

acrylic medium

acrylic paint

black marker

corkboard

19-gauge craft wire

E-6000 glue

E-Z-Cut carving block

fabric or paper scraps

glue stick

1" (2.5cm) wide grosgrain ribbon

packing tape or felt

pencil (2B or softer)

Ranger Distress Crackle Paint

3 2" × 3" (5cm × 7.5cm) resin frames

scrap paper

spray paint (optional)

typing paper

wire words made from 16-gauge dark annealed steel wire: *create*, *dream* and *inspire* (see page 19, Steps 1 and 2)

Finishing the Project

butterfly rubber stamp

cork sheet

metal keyhole

polymer clay

TOOLS

awl

block-cutting tool

foam brush

heat gun

needle-nose pliers

paintbrush

rubber brayer

scissors

sandpaper

wire cutters

TECHNIQUES

Creating a Custom Stamp

Distressing a Corkboard Frame

Adding Decorative Elements

Fold a piece of typing paper in half. Using a soft lead pencil (2B or softer), sketch half a symmetrical design along the fold line.

Unfold the paper and then fold it again so the sketch is pressed against the blank half of the paper. Rub the back of the sketch side to transfer the design to the blank side, completing the image.

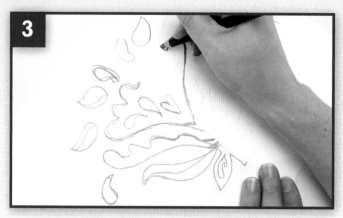

Using the soft pencil, trace over the complete image. Press the image into the surface of the E-Z-Cut block and rub. Your design should transfer clearly to the block.

Using a block cutter, remove the negative space surrounding the design by carving it from the block.

Tip

Use a black marker to color in the parts of the design you want to carve out. Remember to always cut away from yourself to avoid injury!

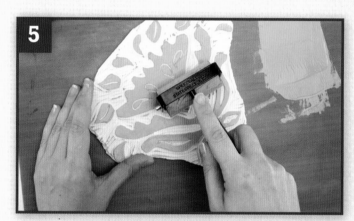

Using a rubber brayer, roll acrylic paint onto the stamp, making sure to cover it completely. Press the stamp facedown onto the corkboard surface. Leave ¼ of the board on the right-hand side unstamped.

Use sandpaper to rough up the surface of the corkboard frame. Place a piece of scrap paper under the frame and on top of the cork to protect the cork surface from accidental drips. Using a foam brush, paint the frame with 1 to 2 coats of acrylic paint. Let the paint dry. Apply a coat of Ranger Distress Crackle Paint in a complementary color, leaving some areas unpainted. Use a heat gun to dry the paint and induce crackles. Seal the frame with an acrylic medium.

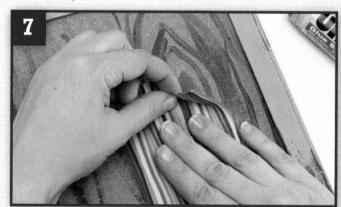

On the unstamped section, use a paintbrush to paint a wood-grain design with watered-down acrylics. Let the paint dry. Remove the backs from 3 resin frames. Cut scraps of fabric or paper slightly larger than the frame openings and use a glue stick to adhere them over the wood-grain design in the desired positions. Using E-6000 glue, adhere the frames over the fabric or paper backgrounds.

8

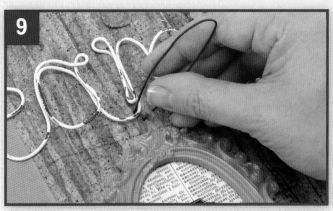

9

Cut a piece of 1" (2.5cm) wide grosgrain ribbon as long as the width of the board and glue it to separate the stamped corkboard from the painted corkboard section. Take out your previously made wire words *create*, *dream* and *inspire* (see page 19, Steps 1 and 2). (You can use the templates on page 124 to create them.) Paint the wire words with spray paint if desired and let them dry. Position the wire words on the board as desired. Hold a word in position and use an awl to poke a hole on either side of the wire in several places throughout the word so it will be secured adequately to the board. Repeat this step for the remaining wire words.

Bend 3"–4" (7.5cm–10cm) pieces of 19-gauge wire in half to create tight U shapes. Push the ends of the wires through a pair of securing holes made in Step 8. Pull the wire snug over the wire word. Twist the wire ends together behind the board and then bend them flat against the back of the board. Attach all the words to the corkboard using the same method. Use packing tape or felt to cover the twisted wire ends on the back of the board. This will prevent the wire from scratching your walls.

Finishing the Project

To add to the "inspired" nature of your inspiration board, you can add elements that represent your personal inspirations. I chose to include a butterfly, a keyhole and a heart with wings. To create the butterfly, stamp a rubber-stamp image of a butterfly on a sheet of cork. Cut around the shape, and stitch on a wire butterfly body (see page 66, Step 2). Glue the butterfly and keyhole embellishments in place with E-6000 glue. The winged heart can be created with polymer clay and wire. To make, condition the clay and shape it into a heart. Use 19-gauge wire to form two little wings (see page 116, Step 5). Press the wings into the back of the heart and then bake as instructed. Let the clay cool. Using an awl, poke two holes ¾" (2cm) apart through the board, inside one of the frames. Twist a 6" (15cm) length of the 19-gauge wire around the wings and insert the ends through the holes in the cork. Twist the ends behind the board to secure. Feel free to substitute your own imagery or charms to represent your personal inspirations.

"THE ARTIST IS A RECEPTACLE FOR EMOTIONS THAT COME FROM ALL OVER THE PLACE: FROM THE SKY, FROM THE EARTH, FROM A SCRAP OF PAPER, FROM A PASSING SHAPE, FROM A SPIDER'S WEB."
— PABLO PICASSO

CHAPTER 3

Peeking Over the Fence

Inspirations from Observation

Artists are visual. We're inspired by what we see, and every so often we'll peek over a fence just to see what's on the other side. We'll take a walk through a craft show or peruse an online collection of art just for inspiration. We often end up feeling a bit like voyeurs.

Why do we feel this way? If you were a scientist, would you refuse to calculate others' research into your theories? Would you fault a writer for reading the works of other novelists? In the art world, we run into artists all the time who guard their innovations fervently. They put up barbed wire to keep you and anyone else from peeking over their fence. I can relate to this feeling of propriety. Making the choice to write this book and to share some of my techniques was a difficult one. I realized what I needed to do was ask myself if I wanted to be generous and encouraging to other artists, or isolated in an effort to protect my work. By choosing the first option, I freed myself from the "Me versus You" mentality that so many artists feel. Fortunately for all of us, there are currently many artists willing to give generously of their time, work and experiences through their blogs. They are encouraging all of us to peek over their fences.

Sometimes taking that peek might be all we need to discover a new love or direction of our own. When my husband and I bought our house, we were both immediately frustrated by the backyard. It was a big and boxy space devoid of any creativity or visual interest. We couldn't imagine it any other way until we peeked over the fence at our neighbor's yard. He had the same size yard, with the same soil and same back fence, but his yard had a parklike beauty we loved. Suddenly we could visualize the possibilities.

In order to make a unique work of art, we must combine our knowledge of new techniques with our own inspirations so we are able to look at something we've made and know it's a true reflection of ourselves. It's only when I've combined a technique I've learned with my own inspiration that I feel I've made something amazing.

Inspiration isn't always easy to find. This last year I've been paying attention to my moments of inspiration and attempting to find the source. I discovered it in my own artistic personality, which, as it turns out, is a split personality. One is called the Observer; the other is the Experimentalist. Each finds inspiration in different places and through different means. Moreover, these two personalities are present in each of us. In this chapter and the next, we'll peek into the worlds of the Observer and the Experimentalist to find out what makes each special and worthy of our cultivation. We'll also examine ourselves to discover more about our own artistic personalities.

The Observer

Observers are extremely sensitive to the world around them and gain inspiration in the details. They might see an unusual color combination that inspires them or feel a soft and cuddly object that spurs them to create. For these artists, a trip to the art museum or a hike through the woods is extremely inspiring, and they gain a lot of creative energy from these outings.

As we delve a bit into the Observer's world, we find these artists often have a highly developed ability to visually discern and appreciate the small beauties in the world around them. Claude Monet is one artist who carries the mantle of the Observer well. Monet would bring multiple canvases with him when he went out, and as he observed the light change over the course of a day, he would switch out one painting for another, thereby creating a visual record of the differences in value, tone, light and shadow as the sun's position changed. Monet once wrote, "The only merit I have is to have painted directly from nature with the aim of conveying my impressions in front of the most fugitive effects." From this, I began to think about observation in art. If I looked closely at something, what would it inspire in me? Did it matter what I was looking at?

Over the years, I've explored other visual images, including the human figure, with great interest, but, like a homing pigeon, I find myself returning to images of mountains, waterfalls and flowers over and over again. I feel a soul connection with this imagery that I don't feel with other subject matter like oceans or animals. Part of discovering your artistic personality is to recognize your personal imagery. I don't know why I feel a connection to some things rather than others, but I know they never fail to calm, inspire and captivate me. In your role as Observer, you might find yourself fascinated by the texture of tree bark, wild grasses, weather patterns, the look of lace or handblown glass. Express your personal imagery—including those details others might not notice—through your art. Give others the gift of appreciating something as you do. Let them peek over your fence to share your vision.

Cultivating Inspiration

Collecting

When we collect tokens of our inspirations in a sketchbook or on an inspiration board, we're creating a visual resource we will be able to use again and again. These tokens might be a paint sample or an amazing photo. Try taking a walk this week. Pay attention to your surroundings as you walk and collect the images you see. This could be as simple as looking down and picking up a leaf or a rock with an unusual streak. It might mean taking your sketchbook or journal and pausing to sketch or describe something you see. Alternatively, you could take your camera to snap a few photos. Paste these photos in your sketchbook and jot a note about what interested you about that image. Pin a couple to your inspiration board. Soon you'll begin to see—reflected in your collection—the colors, textures or imagery your artistic personality enjoys. Sometimes your thoughts about an object might provide a valuable clue.

Coffee Conversational Photo Holder

Imbued with an aroma that instantly comforts me, this piece evokes memories of coffee-shop evenings spent enriching my soul through conversations with kindred spirits. I love to sketch or write at my desk and enjoy the rich scent of coffee beans or catch a glimpse of the inspiration this cup holds. I tuck bits of paper with inspirational quotes, old photo postcards or found ephemera into the wire spirals—anything I take pleasure in seeing or that sparks some inspiration.

You, too, can create your own coffee cup photo holder with a little plaster, a cup and saucer, and some wire! Make one for yourself and you'll see how simple this is. Then make more for all your coffee-lovin' friends!

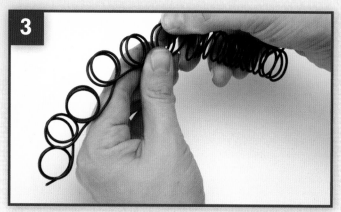

Spread out the coils by bending them flat, 2 at a time, leaving a small space between each pair. Continue this pattern to the end of the coil or until your length matches the height of your pages. Trim any excess wire.

Stack the cover and fabric pages together and then fold them in half. Place a straightedge in the center crease of the top page and mark every inch with a pencil. Start from the center and mark in each direction to ensure symmetrical spacing.

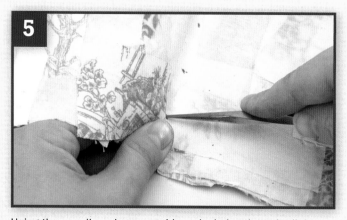

Using the pencil marks as a guide, poke holes through all the pages with an awl.

Knot the end of a 24" (61cm) piece of embroidery floss or heavy-duty cotton thread and, using a needle, begin to stitch through the page layers. Place the wire accent from Step 2 at the outside fold line. As you stitch the pages together, stitch the wire to the outside spine as well. When you reach the end of the book, turn it around and continue to stitch back to the other side. Knot and trim the thread.

Finishing the Project

Now's the time to reach for those mixed-media supplies! Once my pages were stitched, I began to fill the pages with doodles, decorative stitching, buttons, tulle and anything else that looked fun. I also created a clasp for the book by stitching a button to the middle edge of the cover and a strip of fabric to the corresponding spot on the back cover. I tied fabric strips to the wire spine of the book. I printed out photos of my favorite places onto photo fabric to fill my pages. I also printed out a journal entry I'd written and placed cut-up pieces of it throughout the book. To embellish the photos and journal entries I added collage elements such as fiber, tags and torn pages from vintage books. After adding some stickers and art stamps around the photos, it was finished!

CHAPTER 4

Forcing Growth

Using Challenges to Introduce New Techniques and Mediums

One of my favorite purchases in late winter is a bulb garden. I love watching the new shoots burst forth from the soil and grow and bloom on my kitchen table, especially because my garden outside is still covered with snow. My tabletop bulb garden blooms earlier because it has been forced to do so. "Forcing growth" is a term that describes the process in which the gardener will chill a planted bulb to simulate winter and then expose it to warmth to induce growth and flowering when desired. As artists, we can use this technique to force ourselves to grow as well. Fortunately, we don't need to chill ourselves to do it; we can induce growth through challenges and experimentation. These experiences stretch our limits and allow us to grow.

In the previous chapter we talked about the Observer's inspirations. In this chapter, I'd like to introduce you to the Experimentalist.

The Experimentalist

Experimentalists love to try new things and make discoveries. They are happiest when learning a new technique or exploring a new medium. Experimentalists are the mad scientists of the art world. They want to know everything about everything and love to find out the answers to their "What if?" questions. They are driven by the process, and the artwork is often just a by-product.

My dad is an Experimentalist cook. He'll make soup and throw anything he finds from the cupboard into the pot. Then he'll add some vegetables, maybe some rice and a dash of this or that—whatever sounds good. He comes up with some amazing soups using this method, though some are amazingly good and some amazingly bad. Whatever the outcome, he just enjoys working with the ingredients. If he discovers a unique taste combination along the way, he's pleased. Just like my dad, I love to mix mediums, and I often make a lot of my discoveries and develop new techniques by combining and experimenting. To do this, you must be open to the idea of trying something new and be willing to channel your inner child and play for the sheer joy of discovering.

Being an Experimentalist often means becoming a beginner again. That can be a frightening place for some of us. It can also be an advantage. When people approach a new skill, such as soldering, or a new craft, such as quilting, they are often less critical of what they make than they might be otherwise. When we are beginners, we're able to turn down the voice of that inner critic and cut ourselves some slack.

However, it doesn't take long before we're examining our beginner work and comparing it to our more experienced work. This is a form of self-sabotage. Artists need to allow themselves to create bad art. It is a learning process we must let ourselves experience.

Protecting Your Seedlings

In the past I would sometimes show my work to people prematurely. I would get excited about a new path I was following and show my work to others, expecting them to admire it. Often, I was met with only blank looks; they just didn't get it. My heart would plummet, and I'd scurry back to my studio, depressed and doubtful. The spark I felt was something only I could see. When this happens, it's important to believe in yourself. Although you, the artist, can see the spark now, others might not see it until it's grown into a blaze. I've learned to protect my seedlings; showing your work to others before it has had time to develop can set you up for defeat. If you really want an honest opinion, show it to an artist friend. Choose someone supportive who will encourage you. Tell her it's something new you're feeling your way toward, and that it's a work in progress. Don't ask for a critique just yet.

Challenging Yourself

If we are willing to experiment, it can expose us to new discoveries. Some of them are fortuitous accidents that end up leading us in a new exciting direction. It's a bit like taking a drive to the seashore with no map to show the way—we'll take the road that seems to lead in the right direction, but often the road curves and takes us somewhere completely different. So, we'll take another road, which again usually ends up going the wrong way. Trying to reach the seashore, we'll suddenly find ourselves in the mountains instead. It's frustrating, and we're apt to criticize ourselves, but then we notice that in the distance, we can see the sea. The wrong ways were frustrating but were an important part of our progress. Without them, we wouldn't have reached the mountaintop, and our vision would not have cleared. We'd still be driving around the valley without knowing which way to go next.

I often have an idea of where I might want to take a project, but I have no notion of how to execute it. I strike out in the direction that seems best, and when it doesn't take me where I want to go, I try another path. Each time, I discover what doesn't work, but I gain one more clue of what will. Though my choices rarely lead me exactly where I want to go, when they do, I feel as if I've been given a gift. More often, the process takes patience and a realization that sometimes getting lost can mean finding your way.

If you've been feeling a little stuck lately, you may find a burst of inspiration by searching for something new. Give wire and fabric a try and stretch yourself in a new way. Artist challenges are another great way of digging yourself out of a rut. Many magazines and websites offer reader challenges that are meant to inspire. They usually present guidelines and limitations to provide you some direction, and most have deadlines that will motivate you to get it done. A few years ago, a friend of mine mentioned a new magazine, *Sew Somerset*, that she thought I might like. As I glanced through the articles and gallery pages, it occurred to me that I could do this, too. My style was slightly different than what I saw in the magazine, but I really felt I could create something to submit.

I took a chance and submitted one of my wire and fabric flowers, and a wire heart with wings, along with a few article proposals. The night I got an e-mail stating that one of my proposals had been selected, I literally started jumping up and down. It was an awesome feeling and was well worth the chance I had taken. Since then I haven't always been successful with my submissions, but I still believe it's worth it to extend yourself and take a chance. Seek out a challenge you feel inspired by. It's a great way of forcing yourself to grow as an artist.

Trying something new, taking on the

Create Your Own Recipe for Mixed-Media Inspiration

This is a simple but fun way to challenge yourself. It came to me as I was watching an episode of *Top Chef*. Each reality show contestant was given the same set of ingredients. They were also allowed to add one or two "wild card" ingredients. Then they would all make something unique and amazing. Inspired by the creativity of the contestants, I made my own mixed-media recipe challenge. You can, too. Just write down the following recipe and choose your own "ingredients."

Recipe for Mixed-Media Inspiration

Ingredients:

1 color palette: Choose any 2 colors to work with.

1 new medium: Try something you've never tried before.

1 substrate: Be adventurous and choose something you don't usually work with, such as fabric, wood, Plexi, foam or canvas.

2 "wild card" ingredients: These can be mediums you're already familiar with, additional colors or extra materials.

Select ingredients and write them down in your sketchbook. Take a few minutes to write or sketch out your initial ideas. Then gather your materials. Set aside some time to work and then mix all ingredients together. Combine thoroughly on the substrate. Experiment as necessary. Continue working until you're satisfied that your art is complete.

Yields: 1 unique piece of art

role of the beginner, letting yourself create uncensored and choosing to challenge yourself are all ways to grow your art and cultivate inspiration in your life. We trigger energy and excitement when we try something new, and it can be harnessed into creative energy if you channel it correctly. Try taking up the mantle of the Experimentalist. Be daring. Indulge in those flights of fancy, travel down a new path or pick up a book on an unfamiliar medium. Sign up for a workshop or retreat that sounds a little scary but wonderful, too. Any of these suggestions will force your growth and cause your garden to flourish in unexpected ways. Just be brave and experiment!

In the spring, I often wake to the happy trills and whistles of the birds as they sing their morning songs. One particular morning I listened to their cheerful calls and felt my heart fill with the desire to create. I went immediately to my studio room, grabbed a piece of hardboard I'd set aside and started to collage.

The art from that session resulted in the *Birdhouse Assemblage*. To create this piece, I departed from the fabric and canvas I usually used and opted instead for hardboard. In the process I learned how to construct a dimensional wooden substrate, how to attach wire to this substrate and how to create clay tiles to accent my work. The result is a distressed, layered and textured piece I know you'll be pleased to display.

MATERIALS

- acrylic alphabet stamps
- acrylic paint
- colored pencils
- 16-gauge dark annealed steel wire
- embroidery floss
- fabric scraps
- fiberfill stuffing
- glue stick
- ink pad
- Inktense pencils
- nails
- oil crayons
- paper scraps
- 11½" × 19" (29cm × 48cm) piece of hardboard
- polymer clay in light brown, dark brown and turquoise
- pottery glaze in brown
- scrapbooking paper
- tree branches or twigs
- used carpenter's ruler
- water-soluble crayons
- wire word made from 19-gauge craft wire: *home* (see page 19, Forming Words from Wire, Steps 1 and 2)
- 1" × 2" (2.5cm × 5cm) wood scrap, 12" (30.5cm) long
- yarn

TOOLS

- bamboo skewer
- book roughly the same width as the wood scrap (to stabilize while hammering)
- clay knife
- craft drill with ⅛" (3mm) bit
- flat-nose pliers (optional)
- foam brush
- hammer
- needle-nose pliers
- round tube for rolling out clay
- scissors
- sewing needle
- silicone mat
- superglue
- toothpick
- wire cutters

TECHNIQUES

Constructing and Collaging a Unique Substrate

Sculpting a Wire Bird

Stitching and Stuffing the Bird

Adding Embellishments

"Not to put too fine a point on it/Say I'm the only bee in your bonnet/Make a little birdhouse in your soul."

— THEY MIGHT BE GIANTS, "Birdhouse in Your Soul"

With a glue stick, randomly attach a variety of torn paper scraps to cover the hardboard surface. Try sheets of music, junk mail, scrapbooking papers, old handwritten letters, packaging labels—whatever appeals to you.

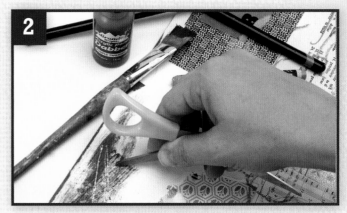

Doodle on the collaged surface with mixed-media art supplies such as acrylic paints, Inktense pencils, colored pencils, oil crayons and water-soluble crayons. Occasionally rough up the surface by peeling off some of the paper or scratching it with scissors.

Drill a hole about 1" (2.5cm) in on each top corner. Working from the spool, insert 16-gauge wire through the back of the left corner hole. Pull the wire through 3" (7.5cm) and over the top of the board, wrapping it around itself to secure. Run the wire across the length of the board and cut the wire 7" (18cm) past the edge. Pull the wire through the other hole and wrap as before. Trim the wire.

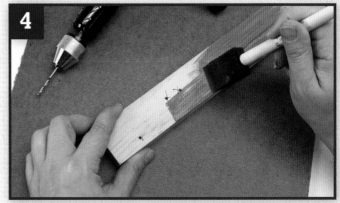

Place a 1" × 2" (2.5cm × 5cm) wood scrap horizontally so the 2" (5cm) side is lying flat on a surface you can drill on. Then use the drill to create holes for the wire bird, nest and branches to be attached with wire later. Drill 3 holes along the bottom edge of the wood for the branches to attach to. One hole should be on each end, 1" (2.5cm) in from the edge, and the third hole should be positioned between the other 2 holes. Drill another 2 holes side by side ¾" (2cm) apart, roughly positioned 3" (7.5cm) in from the left edge of the wood, and 1" (2.5cm) from the bottom. These are to attach the bird and nest later. Paint the piece using acrylic paint and a foam brush. Let the paint dry.

5

Flip the hardboard over so the collage side is facing down. Support the top part of the board with a book that is roughly the same width as the wood scrap. Position the wood so the 1" (2.5cm) edge is flush against the bottom edge and the right or left side of the piece. (See tip below for advice on positioning.) Make sure the edge that has been drilled with the 3 holes is positioned facing out and not against the hardboard. Nail the wood to the hardboard.

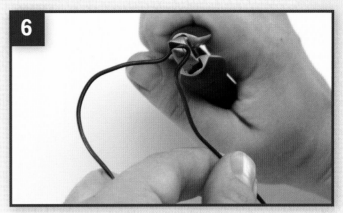

6

Working from the spool, use pliers to bend 16-gauge wire 5"–6" (13cm–15cm) from the cut end to form a beak. Shape the head and back of the bird with your hands and then make a *U* shape for the tail. Bring the wire to the cut end again to form the rest of the bird's body.

Note: *For Steps 6–8 you can also use the template on page 122 as a guide.*

Tip

If the wood scrap is on your left while nailing, it will be on the right once it is flipped back over. If the wood scrap is on your right while nailing, it will be on the left once it is flipped back over.

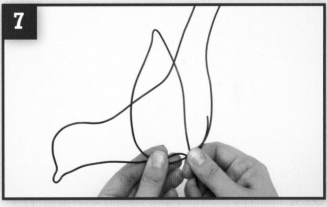

7

At the bottom of the bird, bend the wire up and shape 1 wing.

8

After shaping the wing, return to the bottom of the bird and twist the ends together several times. Cut the wire, leaving 5"–6" (13cm–15cm) excess to attach the bird to the wood scrap. Twist the tail once. The finished bird should measure approximately 9" × 10½" (23cm × 27cm).

9

To add fabric to the wire frame, first use embroidery floss to stitch a piece of scrap fabric, slightly larger than the wing shape, to the wire wing. Trim around the shape, leaving a ¼" (6mm) allowance. Select 2 pieces of fabric slightly larger than the shape of the bird and, holding wrong sides together, position the fabric beneath the wire form. Using embroidery floss, stitch both pieces to the wire body of the bird, leaving a 2" (5cm) opening to insert stuffing. Complete the body of the bird only—the tail is stitched separately. Stuff the bird, using a bamboo skewer to fill in tight spaces. Stitch the opening closed. Trim the fabric, leaving a ¼" (6mm) allowance around the wire. Repeat this step for the tail.

10

Take out your previously made wire word *home* (see page 19, Steps 1 and 2). (You can use the template on page 123 to create it.) Press the wire word gently into a rolled-out piece of polymer clay. Add dots of clay in a contrasting color, poking each dot with a toothpick. Form eggs from turquoise and light brown clay, using a toothpick to make little speckle marks all over the eggs. Form a heart from turquoise clay, and use a toothpick to poke a hole through the top. Create tiles by rolling out clay and stamping or marking as desired. Cut the rolled clay into small squares to create tile shapes. Assemble all clay elements on a silicone mat and bake following the manufacturer's instructions.

11

Insert the bird sculpture's excess wire through the triangle of holes in the scrap wood, bending the ends under. Attach twigs to the front of the perch by running wire through the holes drilled along the edge in Step 4. Coil wire in a tight circle, slowly building upward and outward to create a wire nest. Attach the nest with more wire in front of the bird. Break a carpenter's ruler into several pieces: 2 7" (18cm) lengths and 1 14" (36cm) length that folds in the middle. Form the roof of a birdhouse with the 14" (36cm) piece and the 2 sides with the 7" (18cm) pieces. Use superglue to adhere them to the board on the opposite side of the bird and perch.

12

13

Insert a small piece of wire through the hole in the clay heart and attach it to a twig or branch. Apply a brown pottery glaze to the clay eggs to bring out the speckled texture. Glue these into the nest with superglue.

Cut out cloud shapes from fabric and sew a running stitch around them with a contrasting color of embroidery floss. Adhere the clouds to the board with a glue stick.

Using acrylic alphabet stamps and ink, stamp a phrase or quote onto a piece of scrapbooking paper. I stamped *one bird, one branch, one morning song*. Tear around the paper to give it rough edges and use a glue stick to attach it just above the bird's tail. Wrap small sticks together with yarn and glue this bundle above the list. Using superglue, adhere the tiles around the list.

14

Create a wire circle to fit inside the roof portion of the birdhouse. Cover the circle with fabric on each side, wrong sides together, and stitch the fabric to the wire, leaving a 2" (5cm) space for stuffing. Stuff the circle and stitch the opening closed. Use superglue to attach the circle inside the birdhouse roof.

Altered Canvas Bag

When I started working on this canvas bag, I brought it to the point where I'd stitched on the word *inspired*, and I really liked the result. My original vision, however, had also included free-form brainstorming bubbles drawn in permanent ink. When the time came to actually write on the bag, I hesitated. It seemed so permanent and so easy to mess up. The moment called for courage. I knew that in the end I wouldn't be satisfied with the bag as it was, so I took a deep breath, checked my sketch and—with permanent marker in hand—began to draw.

This project will stretch you, either because you're sharing your own free-association thoughts with others or because you're writing directly on your surface. Don't worry about your handwriting; it doesn't have to look pretty. Just be brave, trust yourself and be willing to push yourself just a little farther. Take a chance and do what it takes to make your bag not just good, but great!

MATERIALS

black fine-tip
permanent marker

embroidery floss

fabric paint markers

fusible interfacing

large canvas bag with
a lining

paper

pencil

wire word made
from 19-gauge dark
annealed steel wire:
inspired (see page
19, Steps 1 and 2)

Finishing the Project

*Blooming Flower Key
Chain* (see page 14)

buttons

charms

old keys

silk flowers

TOOLS

iron

ironing board

scissors

sewing needle

TECHNIQUES

Stitching a Wire Word
to a Bag

Adding Designs to a
Bag's Exterior

Adding
Embellishments

Closing the Slit in the
Lining

Notes on the Process

With this project I became very aware of negative and positive spaces. It was tempting to jam every inch of the bag with doodled text. In any project we do we need to be aware of the balance of positive and negative spaces. The eye will fatigue if you don't leave it a place to rest, and the viewer will turn away to find relief elsewhere. The addition of 3-D elements really helps complete the composition by breaking up the sections of text.

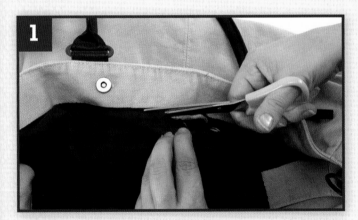

Carefully cut a 5" (13cm) slit in the bag's lining at the inside top edge, on the front of the bag. Cut as close to the top edge of the lining as possible.

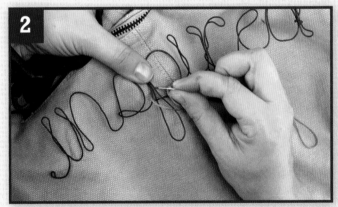

Take out your previously made wire word, *inspired* (see page 19, Steps 1 and 2). (You can use the template on page 124 to create it.) Holding a needle threaded with embroidery floss, insert your hand through the opening. With your other hand, hold the wire word where you want to attach it to the outside of the bag. Begin basting the word to the bag's exterior. Be careful not to stitch through the lining.

"Never leave a painting mediocre; it's better to take a chance with it."
— GUY CORRIERO

Switch floss colors as you continue to stitch down the word. This is primarily for effect, but the extra stitching does help prevent the wire from catching on other objects.

Sketch out free-association brainstorming bubbles on paper, using the word *inspired* as a starting point. Reference this sketch to draw the thought bubbles onto the bag with a black fine-tip permanent marker. Continue to draw circles, arrows or any other doodled designs on your bag.

Tip

Your handwriting doesn't have to look perfect for this project. These bubbles are supposed to look as if you drew them spontaneously, directly onto the bag. A "sketched-out" look also adds energy to your design.

Embellish the brainstorming bubbles, circles and arrows with fabric paint markers in assorted colors. Feel free to continue doodling with the markers as desired.

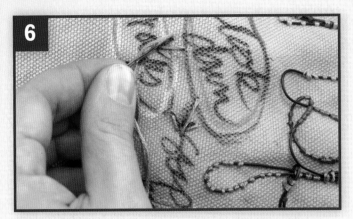

6

Add accent stitches with various colors of embroidery floss around some of the words and doodles. You can also stitch on any found objects or other 3-D elements at this time (see Finishing the Project below). As you add stitching and 3-D elements, make sure to stitch through the canvas only, not the lining.

7

Fold in the top edge of the lining where it was cut. Create as small a fold as possible. Press the fold with an iron. Cut a 1" (2.5cm) wide strip of fusible interfacing that is slightly longer than the opening. Place the strip directly below the cut, between the exterior and the lining. Follow the manufacturer's instructions to iron the opening closed.

Finishing the Project

Choosing to add some 3-D elements such as silk flowers, old keys, buttons, and charms really adds to the uniqueness of your bag. Something as simple as adding the *Blooming Flower Key Chain* from chapter 1 (see page 14), a ribbon pull or your own key fob can imbue your accessory with that designer feel. Or you could decide to push the graffiti feel with some judiciously applied paint splatters or stamp marks. It's all about making something you love and that expresses who you are and what inspires you. So go a little crazy, push your limits and make your bag an original!

Spring is my favorite season. Watching it arrive is always a treat. The snow melts, the trees bud and flowers appear all within two months. It's a time of transformation, and it fills me with excitement and expectations.

When the flowers begin to bloom, it truly feels like an awakening to me. I feel a quickening of my spirit, as if I were a butterfly coming out of my cocoon. This mixed-media piece is a reflection of that feeling. Against a dark background I've placed scraps of fabrics that fairly sing of spring with their bright yellows and greens.

MATERIALS

acrylic metal paint

acrylic paint

24-gauge copper wire

embroidery floss

fabric scraps

fabric strips

glue dots

glue stick

ink pad

4" × 5½" (10cm × 14cm) piece of 36-gauge copper embossing metal

10" × 20" (25.5cm × 51cm) primed canvas

dull scissors for cutting copper embossing metal

foam brush

masking tape

paintbrush

scissors

sewing needle

small bowl with soapy water

wire cutters

TOOLS

acrylic alphabet stamps

acrylic stamps

awl

TECHNIQUES

Appliquéing on Canvas

Stamping on a Metal Sheet

Stitching a Metal Sheet to Canvas

Notes on the Process

After painting the background, I decided to cut the shapes of the flowers as I worked. I prefer to cut each shape individually, without the use of a pattern or stencil. For me, choosing how to cut my shapes is akin to the painter making his presence known through his choice of brushstroke or palette knife. Some artists prefer to absent themselves from a piece by concealing their brushstrokes. We can't see how they applied their color and can't sense the rhythm of their marks. I like to see the hand of the artist in his work. So, instead of cutting perfect little petals that all look the same, I cut each by hand. As a result, each one is different, and I end up with a work that has obviously been made by hand. I see this as an asset to my art rather than a detriment. In my mind, "perfect" is equivalent to "mass-produced."

"Let us learn to appreciate there will be times when the trees will be bare, and look forward to the time when we may pick the fruit."

— ANTON CHEKHOV

Using acrylic paints and a foam brush, paint background colors onto the canvas. Let the paint dry. Cut out stem, leaf and flower shapes from fabric and play around with the composition until you achieve your desired effect. Use a glue stick to tack down the fabric pieces onto the canvas.

Using a needle and embroidery floss, outline and secure each fabric piece to the canvas with a straight stitch. View this stitching process as adding another element of design to your piece—be creative! Add any stamped images and additional painting. Stitch or glue on 3-D objects, such as buttons or old earrings, in the centers of the flowers.

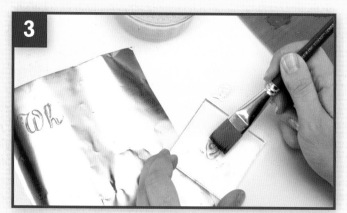

With a paintbrush, apply acrylic metal paint onto alphabet stamps and then stamp them onto a 4" × 5½" (10cm × 14cm) piece of copper embossing metal, creating a phrase or quote. I used *When flowers bloom, my heart awakes.* Be careful not to smear your letter by moving your block as you apply. If you do make a mistake, simply wipe the paint off your sheet immediately and restamp. After you use each letter, peel it off the block and immediately place it into a bowl of soapy water. This prevents the paint from drying on your stamp and possibly ruining it. Allow the stamped text to dry.

Tack the copper embossing metal to the canvas with glue dots in the corners to keep the copper in place as you stitch. Use an awl to punch holes through the metal and canvas for stitching. Punch the holes evenly around the copper sheet and at least ½" (1.5cm) from the edge to prevent tearing it.

5

Thread copper wire in and out of the holes, being careful to pull straight up and down so as not to tear the copper metal. After you poke the wire through the last stitch hole, leave 2" (5cm) excess and then cut the wire. Secure the wire end beneath the canvas either by balling it up so it can't be pulled back through or by bending the wire flat against the canvas back and then taping it securely into place with masking tape.

Tip

Instead of stamping with acrylic paint, try using StazOn ink for a similar effect.

"TO FORGET HOW TO DIG THE EARTH AND TO TEND THE SOIL IS TO FORGET OURSELVES."

— MOHANDAS K. GANDHI

CHAPTER 5

Amending Your Soil

Identifying Problems and Finding Creative Solutions

Most gardeners know, or have found out the hard way, that fabulous bloom times are impossible to achieve in poor soil. The soil of a garden is its foundation. It is in your soil that your plant's roots will stretch and grow and be nourished. Soil that is missing minerals or that is too hard or too porous won't allow seedlings to develop into healthy and hearty plants. Amending the soil with organic material will change it from poor and deficient into a lovely, rich material your plants will love.

Designing Your Space

Much like the soil, our surroundings will either nurture us or deplete us. If surrounded by chaos, our artistic dreams will often wither and die. However, surroundings that nurture our souls with vignettes of beauty and art will allow us to grow and develop as artists. This rich soil is the foundation of our artistic gardens, where our dreams are fertilized. What are your surroundings like? How do you feel in your home? Is it a place you can create in, or are you distracted the moment you walk in the door? The goal of having a beautiful home is one that many of us share. Artist or not, we all want a comfortable and inviting sanctuary. However, the reality is often far from this

vision of loveliness, and many of us are so frustrated by the disparity that we give up. We decide that a home of grace and beauty is only possible for those blessed with the talents of an interior designer or the money to hire one.

I'm not an interior designer, but as an artist I've often been called over to friends' houses to help choose a paint color or decide on furniture placement. Every once in a while a friend will murmur something about how she'd love to see my house: "It must be so lovely and artistic!" I'll smile and secretly resolve never to invite her over. My house is a bedlam of mismatched furniture, cluttered art supplies and half-finished renovation projects, all within the lovely package of an early 1980s split-level desperately in need of a complete remodel. No, I am more than happy to drive to wherever my friends are for a get-together or consult if it means they're able to keep their perceptions of my "lovely and artistic" home.

One day, after someone had just commented again on what a lovely house I must have, I looked around my living room and realized no visitor would ever be able to guess that an artist lived there. I simply didn't have anything that said "art." As I stood there, surprised by the revelation, a phrase came to mind. It was a phrase I'd stumbled upon a day or two before as I was playing with some cut-out text from newspapers and magazines, looking for inspiration. I was rearranging, moving and combining different words, hoping to discover something interesting, when my eye caught the word *art* positioned right next to the words *as usual*. I liked the sound of it immediately: "Art as usual." Art should be the usual, I thought. It should be an everyday, live-with-it-casually, have-it-surround-me kind of usual.

As I pondered my personality-starved home and the phrase "Art as usual," it occurred to me that I could make it a goal to immerse my life and surroundings with art. Instead of thinking of my art as an activity resting along the edges of my life, I would allow art to become part of the usual. I could get up, have coffee, do some doodling, wash dishes, work on a sculpture, run an errand and so on throughout the day until I ended it sitting on the couch or in front of the fireplace, stitching in hand. It sounded so lovely, and for the first time, so doable. I kept my Wednesday night studio time but added in all kinds of little art breaks each day. I treated them as part of my everyday routine rather than something special I had to find time for. And you know what? It worked!

Creating art was now a part of my day-to-day routine, but I wanted to make it the usual in my home as well. I had

to make my surroundings reflect my artistic personality by filling them with art. I started by looking at my space and finding parts of it I really didn't like or that I thought were unattractive. I looked for aesthetic problems that would inspire me to find creative solutions. The cold, bare floor inspired me to tear my old T-shirt collection into strips to create a comfy knitted floor rug. I used my wire-working skills to add leaves and branches to a plain black lamp. These became a perch for a little mama bird watching over her nest. Ordinary things became inspired works of art. Every part of the room was an empty canvas. Soon I found myself walking through my home trying to find more problems to inspire creative solutions. I still love to do this. Not only do I find inspiration, but I also simultaneously create a place of beauty, a home that reflects who I am and feeds and comforts my soul through daily contact.

My home is still too cluttered, too disrupted and too mismatched. It is also slowly becoming the "lovely and artistic" space my friends all imagine I live in. I imagine someday it will be my ideal home, a place that seems to hug you as you enter, a warm, comfy, cozy place that will be a retreat to whoever lingers within it. An art-filled environment in which one can live a life where art is the usual.

Cultivating Inspiration

Looking for Problems to Find Opportunities

At the top of a page in your journal, write the following sentence: "To nurture my creativity at its highest level, my ideal surroundings would . . . ." Write whatever comes to mind. Don't censor yourself. Don't bother with correct grammar or even restrict yourself to words if a sketch would express your ideas more effectively. Our goal is to glean whatever ideas and desires you have within you.

With these ideas in mind, walk around your home and look for areas you dislike or even avoid. In what way could you improve it? What could you create to make it a lovelier space? Sketch your ideas. If the area itself is just too daunting, choose one specific item to improve, like a lamp or small window space. Then sketch some ideas for improving it. Changing one element will change everything. It will encourage and inspire you to continue making changes. Before long, you'll be moving on from one small space to the next, and your path will be strewn with new ideas and fresh creations. You'll love it, and, even better, you'll be living in surroundings that will encourage your artistic self to bloom.

Have you ever watched a butterfly in midflight? It bobs slightly up and down, leisurely flitting from one flower to another. It's amazing to think that not long before, that same butterfly was an earthbound caterpillar inching its way along. So often, I've felt like a little caterpillar, ready and wanting to fly but lacking the wings to accomplish it. That's the miracle of transformation. We can develop beyond our current limits. We can grow wings and fly. I love butterflies because they symbolize this transformation so perfectly.

When I first began to create lamps, the bird and butterfly motifs came to mind easily. The act of turning ordinary objects into delightful pieces of art has a bit of transformational magic to it. The change is so easy and simple to achieve, but because it has been done by hand, the result is really one of a kind.

MATERIALS

- black table lamp base, approximately 15"–20" (38cm–51cm) tall
- buttons or beads
- 19-gauge craft wire
- cream lamp shade to fit lamp base
- 16-gauge dark annealed steel wire
- embroidery floss
- fabric pieces
- fabric scraps
- glue stick
- pencil

TOOLS

- awl
- flat-nose pliers
- round-nose pliers
- scissors
- sewing needle
- wire cutters

TECHNIQUES

Creating Small Fabric and Wire Butterflies

Stitching Through the Lampshade

1

Fold a fabric scrap in half and, assuming the fold is the center of the butterfly, cut out a butterfly wing. Unfold the fabric. (You can also use the Small Butterfly template on page 123.) Cut 6 butterflies, varying their sizes slightly from 1½"–2" (4cm–5cm) wide and 2"–3" (5cm–7.5cm) tall.

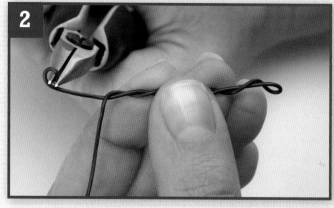

2

Cut a length of 19-gauge wire a little more than twice the height of the fabric butterfly and bend it in half. Twist the wire together, leaving ½" (1.5cm) or so at the end. Using round-nose pliers, turn the ends to form a small spiral shape.

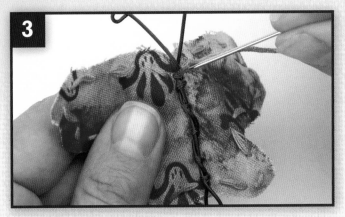

With a needle and embroidery floss, stitch the butterfly's wire body to the center of the fabric shape. Using a contrasting color of floss, straight stitch around the fabric edge, outlining the shape. Using a glue stick, attach butterflies to the lamp shade where desired.

Cut out cloud shapes from fabric scraps and straight stitch around the edge with a contrasting color. Adhere the clouds to the lamp shade with a glue stick.

Using an awl, poke through the shade to mark the butterfly's whimsical flight path. Mark hole placement first with a pencil if desired. Repeat for each butterfly.

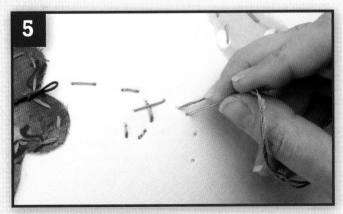

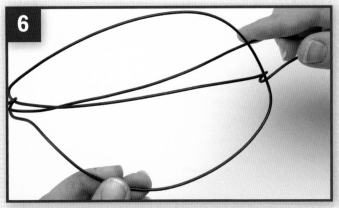

With a needle and embroidery floss, stitch in and out of the holes in the shade to create the flight paths. Knot and trim the floss.

Working from the spool, bend 16-gauge wire approximately 12" (30.5cm) from the cut end to form the center vein and tip of a leaf. Pull the wire around the vein and shape the left side of the leaf. Wrap the wire at the base of the leaf, 4"–5" (10cm–13cm) from the cut end, to create the stem. Form the right side of the leaf and wrap the wire once around the leaf tip. Run the wire parallel to the vein, twist the wire at the leaf base and then run the wire to the bottom of the stem. Cut the wire, leaving 6" (15cm) of excess wire to attach the leaf to the lamp base. Repeat this step to create a second leaf. (You can also use the template on page 125 as a guide.)

"The butterfly counts not months but moments, and has time enough."

— RABINDRANATH TAGORE

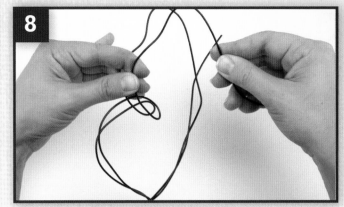

Stitch a fabric piece to each leaf with embroidery floss and trim, leaving a ¼" (6mm) allowance. Working from the spool, coil 16-gauge wire around the lamp, from the top to the base. Bend in the cut ends. Attach the leaves to the lamp, staggering the position so 1 is above the other.

Pull an arm's length of 16-gauge wire from the spool. Bend the wire back on itself and twist it loosely toward the cut end, leaving 3"–4" (7.5cm–10cm) of wire at the cut end for the antennae. Shape 1 wing, twisting the wire once halfway down the wing to create an indentation. Twist the wire around the bottom of the body once to secure. Begin shaping the second wing, using the first wing as a guide and creating the same loop halfway up the wing. Unfold the wings and cut the wire from the spool, leaving 3"–4" (7.5cm–10cm) of excess wire for the second antenna. Twist the antennae together a few times to secure and trim them to the same length. Use round-nose pliers to make loops at the ends of the antennae. Use flat-nose pliers to make small adjustments in the butterfly shape. (You can also use the Large Butterfly template on page 123 as a guide.)

Tip

Because the butterfly is a large shape, you might want to make a few basting stitches along the wire to ensure your fabric doesn't move out of position as you stitch. Remove the stitches as you come to them.

Stitch fabric pieces to each wing separately with embroidery floss, and trim, leaving a ¼" (6mm) allowance. Add contrast stitching to the butterfly's wings, and sew on buttons or beads to embellish it. Stitch the center of the butterfly to the center vein of the leaf.

Two Birds on a Branch

Inspiration often comes to us when we least expect it. I was helping my mother sort through her old teaching supplies one day when I came across a 1950s primary schoolbook on birds. Within the pages were birds in nests, birds on branches, birds in flight—all charmingly illustrated. I wondered if I could use wire to capture the forms of these birds. It took many attempts, but in the end the cute little backward-glancing bird became one of my absolute favorites!

Another artist suggested I make some jewelry displays. I took up the challenge and came up with *Two Birds on a Branch*. This display can be used as intended for jewelry, or it could hang in your kitchen to hold pot holders and utensils. No matter where you put it, these sweet little birds will guard your treasures with handcrafted style.

MATERIALS

- birch branch, approximately 23" (58.5cm) long
- 19-gauge craft wire
- 16-gauge dark annealed steel wire
- embroidery floss
- fabric scraps

TOOLS

- needle-nose pliers
- scissors
- sewing needle
- straightedge
- wire cutters

TECHNIQUES

- Creating Wire and Fabric Leaves and Branches
- Sculpting Wire Birds
- Shaping Wire Hooks

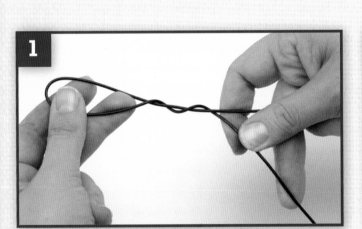

Working from the spool with 16-gauge wire, create a 2" (5cm) loop 10" (25.5cm) from the cut end. Twist the wires together until the twisted section is 4" (10cm) long. This creates a leaf and a branch segment. Use needle-nose pliers to shape points at the ends of the leaves if desired.

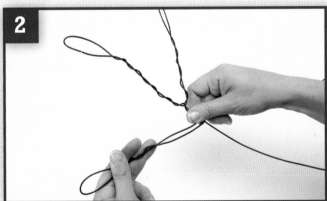

Bend the wire from the spool away from the twist. Create a second 2" (5cm) loop 6" (15cm) away from where the twist ends. Wrap the wire back to the first twist. Continue to loop and twist the wire in this manner to create 5 leaves and branches. Cut the wire from the spool, leaving 6" (15cm) of excess to attach the piece to the birch branch.

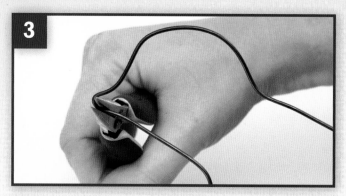

Note: *To create the birds in Steps 3–5, you can also use the templates on page 122 as a guide.*

Working from the spool with 16-gauge wire, begin shaping a backward-glancing bird by creating a slight curvature for the bird's head 14" (35.5cm) from the cut end. Using needle-nose pliers, bend the wire to create the bird's beak and then form the bird's back. Shape the tail and the underside of the bird. Return the wire back to the neck of the bird, just below the first bend.

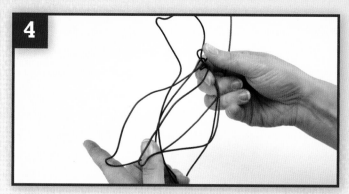

With pliers, bend the wire sharply to the left to create a wing shape. Cut the wire, leaving 12" (30.5cm) of excess. Wrap this wire tightly around the wire at the neck and through the first wing to secure it loosely. Shape the second wing and return the wire to the neck. Wrap the wire tightly around and through the first wing and then cut the wire, leaving enough excess to attach the bird to the branch.

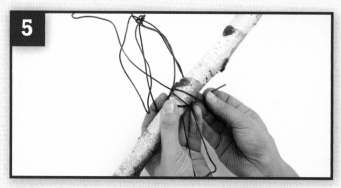

Sculpt a second bird as demonstrated in the *Birdhouse Assemblage* (see pages 51 and 52, Steps 6–8); however, after shaping the first wing, shape a second matching wing on the opposite side of the form. When cutting the wire, leave enough excess to attach the bird to the branch. Attach the birds to opposite sides of the branch with the excess wire.

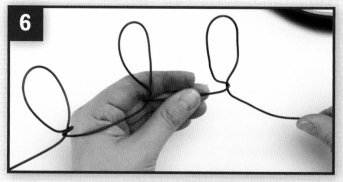

To create hooks, make a 2" (5cm) loop 7" (18cm) from the cut end of the 16-gauge wire. Twist the loop twice, and then straighten the next 2" (5cm) of wire. Continue making these loops, spacing them 2" (5cm) apart, until you have enough loops to fill the length of the birch branch (about 7 hooks). Use a straightedge to ensure the loops are evenly spaced.

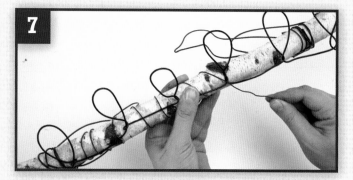

Attach the wire branches to the birch branch, using pliers to wrap the wires securely. To attach the hooks to the branch, hold them against the branch so the hooks stick straight out from the bottom. Pull an arm's length of 19-gauge wire from the spool and, starting from the middle of the branch, wrap it around the branch and the hooks. Once you've reached the cut end, wrap the wire a few more times to secure and then cut off any excess. Return to the middle of the branch and wrap the wire from the spool to the other end. Secure the wire and cut. Bend in the cut ends.

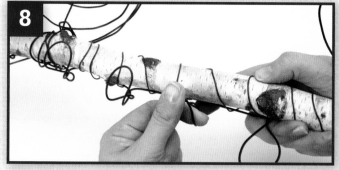

Using your finger or pliers, pinch the center of the hook loops and bend them up. Using a needle and embroidery floss, sew small fabric scraps to the leaves and trim, leaving ¼" (6mm) allowances. To hang this piece, make 2 wire loops and secure 1 at each end of the branch.

Magpie Nest

I don't know how it happens, but I am constantly misplacing (okay, losing) pieces of jewelry. When I look in my jewelry box, I never know if I'll find a pair of earrings or just some broken remnants of whatever it is I'm searching for. I can't bear to throw any of it away—it's all just so pretty and sparkly.

When I created this copper nest, it seemed as if all those pieces finally had a suitable home. Woven into the wire as decorative accents, they glitter and shine beautifully. It reminds me of the magpie, who is known for stealing anything bright or sparkling to line its nest. I wonder if their nests are as beautiful as this one? Isn't it fun to imagine the possibilities?

MATERIALS

beads

20-gauge copper wire

24-gauge copper wire

fabric strips

Finishing the Project

assorted jewelry (old earrings, pins, badges, etc.)

broken colored glass pieces

paper scraps

small silver chain

TOOLS

needle-nose pliers (optional)

scissors

wire cutters

TECHNIQUES

Forming a Wire Nest

Adding Embellishments

Working from the spool, form 20-gauge copper wire into a bowl shape by making a tight spiral and expanding it outward and up. This is similar to creating a coil pot in pottery.

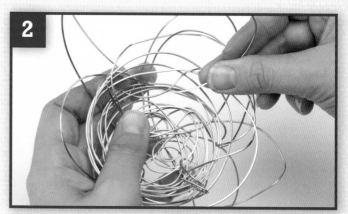

When the nest is the height and width you desire, pull an arm's length of wire from the spool and cut the wire. Begin to wrap and weave the wire through the coils of the nest. Do this in a messy way so it seems more like a nest and less like a patterned bowl. Build up the sides of the nest to make them denser.

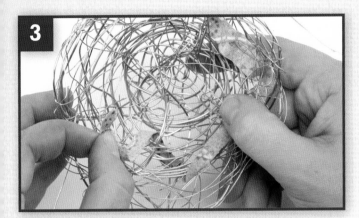

Switch to 24-gauge wire and continue loosely weaving and wrapping the nest. As you weave with the 24-gauge wire, occasionally weave in a small strip of fabric.

Continue to wrap and weave the fabric strips over and around the wire so they are secured in the design. Cut a 10"–12" (25.5cm–30.5cm) length of 24-gauge wire and begin weaving it through the nest, randomly slipping beads onto the wire as you weave and wrap.

Finishing the Project

Once you've formed your nest and worked in color and some sparkle with your fabric and beads, you might want to add other elements as well. A bit of silver chain drapes nicely over the side of the nest, while a few pieces of jewelry add interest and more "bling." My nest has broken pieces of colored glass and bits of paper scribbled with old memories tucked within.

"FASHION IS NOT SOMETHING THAT EXISTS IN DRESSES ONLY. FASHION IS IN THE SKY, IN THE STREET, FASHION HAS TO DO WITH IDEAS, THE WAY WE LIVE, WHAT IS HAPPENING."

— COCO CHANEL

CHAPTER 6

Ornaments for Your Garden

Expressing Your Artistic Personality by Making Your Own Jewelry and Accessories

Gardens are lovely places that impress so many different things upon the visitor. By adding an unexpected twist or turn to the garden path, the garden designer can cultivate a sense of discovery. By using contrasting shapes or bold colors, she imparts a sense of drama. To develop a theme, though, there's nothing like a garden ornament. A garden with a lawn gnome, funky trash sculptures and pink flamingos gives a definite sense of kitschy playfulness, while a serene garden with a pagoda, dry creek bed and stone Buddha invokes a meditative calm. A garden's art expresses the personality of the gardener as much as the garden.

Garden ornaments are considered "bling" for your garden. A shiny reflective orb or sparkling mirrored fountain can adorn a garden the way a diamond bracelet adorns a wrist. Drawing a parallel between garden ornaments and jewelry is easy. Just as the lawn gnome screams kitsch in a garden, the right jewelry can express the personality of the wearer in a way that other, more subtle parts of your wardrobe might not.

Crafting Your Personal Image

I'd like to say my personal style is subtle, but in reality, it's fairly nonexistent. If I find something I like, I'll wear it over and over again. Sadly, neither of these qualities makes me the fashion diva I'd like to be. Every once in a while an occasion comes along that requires me to look a little more dressed up, and then I wonder why I don't do it more often. I resolve to wear something different every day and to actually try to coordinate my clothes, jewelry, shoes and handbag. (I can dare to dream, right?) It never lasts long, though. Coordination seems to require an awful lot of effort, usually in the morning, when I have the least amount of time.

My ideal look is pretty, artistic, bright and unique. For years I wanted to dress in a way that reflected who I was, and I always had a vague desire to look like my art. I knew I didn't want to look like the stereotypical artist dressed all in black. I also knew enough about current styles to realize I was hopelessly out of style. After my son was born, I slipped into the "just trying to survive the day" look. Over the last year, however, I have found a few ways to look more like my ideal image without a lot of effort. Jewelry, I have found, is a fabulous way to "up" the style factor in any outfit. Like garden ornaments, a nice pair of earrings and a fabulous necklace seem to make even my T-shirt-and-jeans combo interesting. I love that jewelry dresses me up and makes me feel chic.

When I plunged into my wire and fabric obsession, it naturally leaked into my other interests. I fell in love with the fabric and fiber cords I created. They're unique and colorful, and when I wear them, I feel like me. I made several in all sorts of colors so I would be able to put one on, no matter what outfit I was wearing. Some had stones for pendants; others had wire and fabric pendants or beads. Each was unique, and all possessed the handcrafted artistic look I love. I began to eye my headbands, hair combs and other accessories as potential candidates for a wire and fiber makeover.

I realized that cultivating a personal style could be just as fruitful a source of inspiration as designing for my home had become. I began to rip out pages from magazines of the clothes I loved and paste them into my sketchbook next to an image of a fabulous painting or room design I'd found. I decided that a beautifully layered vintage French bracelet inspired me in much the same way as did a sculpture fashioned from vintage ceiling tiles. My appreciation for the different and unique hasn't changed, but now I know I can apply that appreciation to my apparel choices. It's one more way to express who I am and what I love. When I wear an outfit or a piece of jewelry that reflects the true "me," my real personality becomes more perceptible to others as well.

I'm not always "in" fashion when I dress this way, but I don't create art to reflect the fashions. I create art that reflects who I am: a lover of bright and pretty objects, and an artist inspired by nature. With a little bit more work, I think my wardrobe could do this, too. A girl's gotta dream, right?

Cultivating Inspiration

Use Your Favorite Mediums and Techniques to Create Wearable Art

Grab a couple fashion magazines or browse online to find some clothes or jewelry you like. Pin your favorite find to your inspiration board. Choose a couple others to put into your sketchbook and try to identify the qualities you like in each photo. Do you like the colors? The way the jewelry is layered? The combination of different metals? The juxtaposition of leather and pearls? If you love period costumes, maybe you'd like to use a book of those as your inspiration source instead of something modern. The idea is to discover what you love.

Once you've figured this out, think about some of your favorite outfits. What do you enjoy wearing? In your sketchbook, sketch some quick ideas of ways you might combine your inspirations and your actual wardrobe. Then give it a shot. Create a cuff or necklace, or embellish a blank canvas bag in whatever style you like. Before long you'll be running errands dressed like the amazingly artistic, fabulously inspired person you are.

Fab Fiber Necklace

For the *Fab Fiber Necklace*, I decided to use a fabric strip to make a cord and came up with a way to stitch around it to create the form I wanted. Once I had the basic form, I wrapped the cord with contrasting fabrics and floss, beautiful fibers and some of my favorite remnants of yarn. After these additions they started to look fairly fabulous. Adding a wire pendant to the center gave the cord a nice drape and created a lovely contrast.

If you've never tried making jewelry before, this is a wonderfully satisfying project to start with. It's fun and easy, and the results are truly fabulous!

MATERIALS

assorted fibers, fabric scraps, embroidery floss and yarn

2 bead caps

19-gauge craft wire

16-gauge dark annealed steel wire

embroidery floss

2 eye pins

1" × 28" (2.5cm × 71cm) fabric strip

fiberfill stuffing

2 6mm silver jump rings

small fabric strips

toggle clasp

TOOLS

bamboo skewer

flush cutters

mandrel with ¼" (6mm) diameter

needle-nose pliers

scissors

2 sets of flat-nose pliers

sewing needle

wire cutters

TECHNIQUES

Creating a Fabric and Fiber Cord

Adding a Clasp to the Cord

Creating Wire Jump Rings

Making a Wire and Fabric Pendant

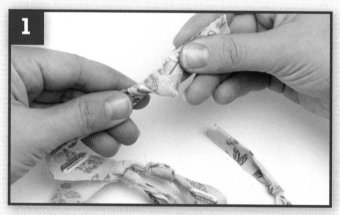

Cut a 1" (2.5cm) wide strip of fabric approximately 28" (71cm) long. Knot the strip occasionally, leaving a ½" (1.5cm) allowance at each end.

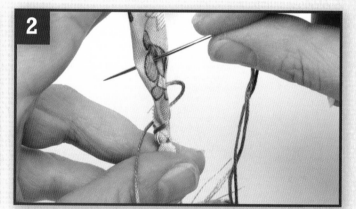

Thread a needle with embroidery floss and knot 1 end about 2" (5cm) from the end. Insert the needle through the first knot and stitch through it a few times to anchor it. Wrap the thread over the front and insert it through the back of the strip, pulling tightly. Continue this every ¾" (2cm) to the end of the strip. Stitch through the last knot a few times to secure. Trim the thread, leaving 6" (15cm) excess.

"Souls wouldn't wear suits and ties, they'd wear blue jeans and sit cross-legged with a glass of red wine."
— CARRIE LATET

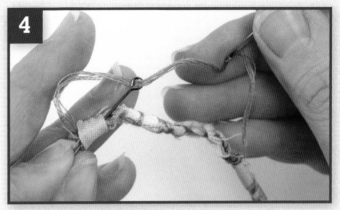

Embellish the cord with assorted yarns, fabric strips, contrasting embroidery floss and other fiber by tying, wrapping and double knotting pieces onto the cord as desired.

Thread the needle with the 6" (15cm) of extra floss at the end of the cord. Insert an eye pin partially through the nearest knot. Sew through the cord and then through the eye pin. Repeat several times to secure.

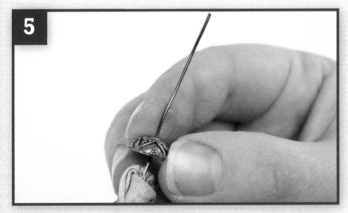

Push the rest of the eye pin through the knot. Thread a bead cap onto the eye pin to partially cover the knot.

With needle-nose pliers, create a small loop where the pin emerges from the bead cap. Wrap the rest of the pin several times beneath the loop. Repeat Steps 4–6 at the other end of the cord.

7

To make jump rings for this and other projects, coil 16-gauge wire around a mandrel with a ¼" (6mm) diameter several times. Slide the coil off the mandrel. You can vary the diameter of the ring by using a smaller or larger mandrel.

8

Cut each coil with flush cutters to make jump rings. Continue to coil and cut wire as described until you have as many as you'd like. (You will need 2 wire jump rings for this project.) Save extra jump rings for other projects.

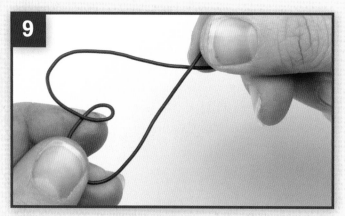

9

Using 19-gauge wire, shape a small heart, beginning and ending at the bottom of the shape. Cut the wire, leaving 2" (5cm) excess.

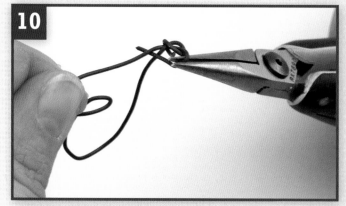

10

Twist the cut ends of the wire a few times to create a point at the bottom and then cut any excess wire closely. Bend in the cut ends of the wire.

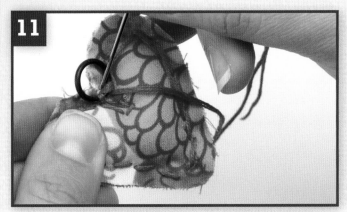

Hold 2 pieces of fabric beneath the wire heart, wrong sides together. With a needle and embroidery floss, stitch the fabric to the wire, leaving a small opening for stuffing. Stuff the heart with fiberfill, using a bamboo skewer to fill in tight spaces. Sew the opening closed. Place a closed wire jump ring behind the pendant at the top of the heart. Sew the wire jump ring to the heart fabric securely with embroidery floss. Attach a second jump ring to the first and then slip it onto the fabric cord. Close the jump ring with flat-nose pliers.

Attach a 6mm silver jump ring to the loop on each end of the necklace. Before closing the jump rings, attach the toggle bar to 1 end and the toggle ring to the other end of the necklace.

It's important to properly open and close jump rings. If you don't, the jump ring will be weakened and possibly pulled out of shape. To do it right, hold a set of flat-nose pliers in each hand and grip each side of the jump ring, with the join centered at the top. Gently twist the join apart, pulling one side back and the other forward. To close, twist the ends again in the opposite direction.

Cloud 9 Cuff

This cuff is a reminder to me of impossible possibilities and the importance of daring to dream them. As artists, when we dream, we need to dream audaciously. To dream audaciously is to dream of impossible things, to dream daringly, to dream boldly. When we dream of the impossible we are allowing ourselves to consider it as a possibility. When we think of something as a possibility, even a wild possibility, we begin to view it as attainable. Make your own *Cloud 9 Cuff* and see it as a personal reminder to dream audaciously of impossible things.

MATERIALS

assorted Czech and seed beads

craft hinge to fit center of cuff

19-gauge craft wire

16-gauge dark annealed steel wire

embroidery floss

fabric scraps

fiberfill stuffing

sewing thread

TOOLS

bamboo skewer

bead needle

needle-nose pliers

scissors

sewing needle

wine bottle or similarly sized object

wire cutters

TECHNIQUES

Creating a Wire Cuff Form

Quilting Fabric to Add Dimension

Adding Beads and a 3-D Object

To create the basic cuff form, wrap 16-gauge wire halfway around a wine bottle or similarly sized object. With the wire still flush against the bottle, form a sideways *U* shape and then run the wire back in the opposite direction. Form a second sideways *U* shape 2" (5cm) from the first *U* shape, and then reverse the wire again, returning to the cut end. Stretch the center of the cuff outward until the width is 2¼" (6cm). Do not cut the wire.

Tip

You can alter the fit of the cuff by using a smaller sized bottle or by wrapping the wire less than halfway around the bottle before looping back.

"Know, first, who you are; and then adorn yourself accordingly."
— EPICTETUS

The wire should now be at the bottom center of the cuff. Gently shape the wire to create an oval shape that outlines the craft hinge. It is helpful to hold the craft hinge against the cuff as you shape. The top and bottom of the oval should be touching the top and bottom wires of the basic cuff form.

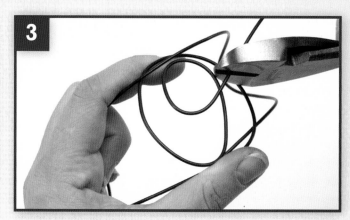

Form the number 9 within the oval shape. Cut the wire and bend in the end with needle-nose pliers.

Wrap 19-gauge wire around the outside of the cuff and the oval shape to secure them together. As you are wrapping around the outside of the cuff, bring the wire from the bottom to the top on either side, forming cloud shapes as you go, and then continue wrapping the outside. Do this twice on both sides of the oval shape.

Place the wrong sides of 2 fabric scraps together and hold them beneath the wire form. Stitch the fabric to the top and bottom of the cuff and then around the center oval shape. Stitch the fabric to the cloud shape to the right of the oval, leaving a slight opening to insert stuffing. Stuff the right side, using a bamboo skewer to fill in tight spaces, and then stitch the opening closed. Repeat the stitching and stuffing process for the remaining cloud shapes. Trim the fabric around the wire, leaving a ¼" (6mm) fabric allowance.

6

Insert the craft hinge so it fits inside the oval, on top of the fabric. Stitch the hinge to the cuff.

Tip

If you can't find craft hinges but want the same look, try cutting your own stamped oval from polymer clay. It makes a great replacement piece!

7

Using a bead needle and sewing thread, stitch seed beads onto the fabric. Be sure to pull each stitch tightly to create indentations that will add more dimension to the cuff.

87

"It's So Charming" Bracelet

When I see charms dangling from someone's wrist, I'm mesmerized for a moment. Each charm is unique and was chosen for a reason. It's a miniature art collection, curated by its wearer. I like to imagine there is a story behind each charm.

The theme I chose for this charm bracelet was inspiration. I created a bracelet with all the major artistic motifs that inspire me. The *P* charm is for the princess dresses I spent hours drawing as a little girl. The bird charm represents nature, by which I am inspired daily. The fabric and wire heart charm is for my family and friends, who constantly surprise and inspire me.

Before you create your bracelet, take a moment to consider your inspirations. Design your bracelet to be reflective of you and your story.

MATERIALS

- acrylic glaze in burnt umber
- bird charm
- craft glue
- 19-gauge craft wire
- clear gel medium
- 16-gauge dark annealed steel wire
- fabric scraps
- light brown polymer clay
- two-part nontoxic clear resin

Finishing the Project

- 8" (20.5cm) bracelet chain
- ceramic, Czech and pearl beads
- handmade wire jump rings (see page 82, Steps 7 and 8)

- head pins
- metal charms

TOOLS

- acrylic stamps
- clear resin kit, as suggested by manufacturer
- craft sheet
- double-sided tape
- flush cutters
- hammer
- mandrel with ½" (1.5cm) diameter
- metal block
- metal jewelry file
- needle-nose pliers
- packing tape
- paper towels
- round-nose pliers
- round tube for rolling out clay

- scrap wood
- silicone baking mat
- scissors
- toothpick
- tweezers
- wire cutters
- wooden craft stick

TECHNIQUES

- Creating a Basic Wire Charm Form
- Creating Clay Charms
- Creating Resin Charms
- Creating a Wire S Clasp

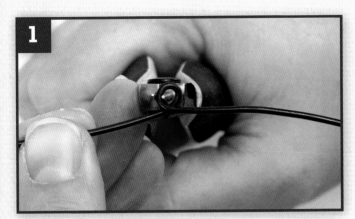

To create a basic charm form, grip a length of 16-gauge wire about 2" from the cut end with round-nose pliers. Wrap the wire around the pliers to create a bail.

Wrap the wire around a mandrel with a ½" (1.5cm) diameter to form a circle beneath the bail. Wrap the wire around the bail. Cut the wire and trim any excess. Make the desired number of basic wire charm forms.

Using a hammer and metal block, flatten the wire so it lies evenly on the surface.

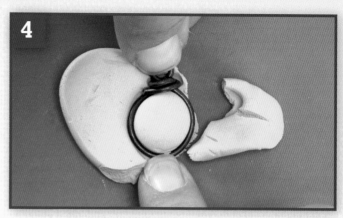

To make a clay charm, condition a small piece of polymer clay and roll it out. Press a basic wire charm form into the clay. Pull the excess clay from the wire and place it on a silicone baking mat.

Using acrylic stamps, imprint designs or words into the clay.

Bake the charm following the manufacturer's instructions. When it has cooled completely, apply burnt umber acrylic glaze over the stamp indentions. Wipe the glaze from the surface with a paper towel, leaving it only in the stamped areas.

To make a resin charm, press a piece of packing tape firmly to the back of a basic wire charm form, rubbing over it with your finger to ensure a complete seal. Set a piece of scrap wood on top of a craft sheet and apply double-sided tape to the top. Place the taped wire charm form onto this sticky surface, positioning it so the bail is hanging over the edge of the wood.

Mix clear resin according to the manufacturer's instructions. Shape a wire heart from 19-gauge wire to fit inside the frame, and cut a fabric scrap roughly the same size. Place the fabric into the resin using tweezers and then place the wire heart on top. Using a craft stick, drip resin into the wire frame, making sure not to overfill the charm. Use a toothpick to pop any bubbles that appear on the surface of the resin. Let the resin cure according to the manufacturer's instructions. You can also make a clear resin charm by omitting the fabric and wire heart.

To create a bird and fabric charm, make a clear resin charm following the instructions in Step 7. Cut a small circle of fabric to fit the back of the cured charm and use craft glue to adhere it onto the back, with the right side against the resin. Remove any loops or connectors from the bird charm with flush cutters, and file off any sharp edges with a metal file. Glue the charm to the front of the clear resin charm with a dab of clear gel medium.

To make a wire S clasp, use needle-nose pliers to bend in the cut end of the wire tightly until it lies flush against the rest of the wire. Using the pliers to grip the center, gently bend the wire to form a loose hook. Cut the wire, leaving an extra 1" (2.5cm) of wire. Shape the extra wire in the opposite direction of the finished S shape.

Finishing the Project

To assemble the bracelet, attach a handmade wire jump ring (see page 82, Steps 7 and 8) to each charm and then attach the charms to an 8" (20.5cm) bracelet chain. Attach the S clasp to one end of the chain with a wire jump ring. Attach a wire jump ring to the other end.

Create dangles for the bracelet using assorted ceramic, Czech and pearl beads threaded onto head pins. After the beads are on the head pins, make a loop at the top with needle-nose pliers and wrap the rest of the head pin around the loop once or twice. Trim the excess wire. Choose metal charms that inspire you. Attach the beaded dangles and charms to the bracelet chain with jump rings.

CHAPTER 7

Creating a Seasonal Garden

Living the Inspired Life Year-Round

Gardens change throughout the year, with seasons bringing different stages of transformation to life. Each season is unique with its own colors and imagery, and I happily anticipate the advent of spring, summer, fall and winter. I find inspiration in the changes they bring. By late summer, I can't wait for the trip to the orchard, hot apple cider and the warm reds, browns and oranges of the fall leaves. By late fall, I'm already looking forward to the blanket of white snow that will cover my yard, making everything pristine and bright. The air is scented with wood smoke and evergreens as we gather in front of the fireplace, hot cocoa in hand. By the time the New Year arrives, I'm already thinking and planning for spring. I use this time for contemplation and renewal. Soon, spring dawns with its small green shoots that promise a fresh beginning. My gardens burst forth in yellows as the first shoots of the forsythia bloom and sleepy daffodils raise their nodding heads. It is an awakening, and I can feel it in my soul. Then, just as spring seems to be exploding around me, summer arrives with its warmth and energy. The garden begins to overflow with produce, and the flowers hang heavy with blooms. As artists, we can use the imagery and colors of each

season, as well as our emotional responses to them, as sources of inspiration for our art.

As I anticipate each seasonal change, I create little vignettes within my home so I'm surrounded by some of the sights, smells and colors of that season. My dining room chandelier is one spot I use for this purpose. I'm able to hang snowflakes and icicles in winter; I can place a nest in it for spring and drape it with a bittersweet garland in fall. I also have paintings I switch out in my living room. When I keep the same art year-round, it ceases to catch my eye, and I don't enjoy it as much. I have since been inspired to create different pieces for different times of the year. My mother-in-law has seasonal quilts she hangs on her walls. Warm browns and reds for fall and winter, and light pinks, greens and browns for the spring and summer months. Everything else in her home remains the same—the furniture, the rugs, the accent pieces—but there's a coziness about the rooms in the cooler seasons and a lovely breeziness each spring and summer.

In your own home you can change as much or as little as you desire, but making some changes not only enhances the sense of anticipation and excitement for the seasons, it also gives us an excuse to work with different images and color palettes. You might naturally gravitate to a pastel palette in your art, but when creating for fall, give the warm hues of red and orange a try. If you love to work with the images of flowers, try using leaves or pumpkins as inspiration. Celebrate the seasons, and you're celebrating the changes in life. You're also connecting your life to the highs and lows of nature.

Each project in this chapter celebrates a different season. A *Fall Leaf Garland* (see next page) made with batik fabrics glows with the richness of fall when placed in front of a window. *Quilted Christmas Ornaments* (see page 98) will give a lovely handmade feeling to your winter celebrations, and a *May Day Cone* (see page 102) crafted from chicken wire and decorated with pearls is a great way to celebrate spring. The *Summer Sun Catcher* (see page 106) channels the warmth and cheerfulness of a summer day. These ideas only scratch the surface of what you can do when you use the changing seasons or holidays as inspiration. Soon you'll be living the inspired life year-round!

Cultivating Inspiration

Creating a Calendar for Inspiration

In your sketchbook or journal, write the names of each season at the top of a page. Then free associate as you sketch or write what images or thoughts come to mind when you think of that season. What colors do you associate with the different times of the year? What activities or images come to mind? Then look at a calendar and note the holidays that fall within each season. Winter, for instance, has Christmas and Valentine's Day, as well as a few others, depending on where you live.

Then write or sketch an idea for a project you could do in response to each season or holiday. You could create a fabric and wire wrist corsage for Mother's Day, a spooky wire tree or quilt for Halloween, a quirky little rabbit for Easter or a stitched "I love you" for Valentine's Day. The projects can be whimsical in nature or just a nod to the season, as my mother-in-law's quilts are. It's up to you how you want to develop your project ideas. Make a note on your calendar or in your day planner to remind you of your ideas. Then, as the season approaches and you have a little spare time, your inspiration will be available with just a glance at your calendar.

Fall Leaf Garland

Each fall is marked by changes in light and color. Brilliant oranges, reds and yellows and deep buttery browns seep into leaves of every shape and size, treating us to a grand finale before the curtain of winter falls. To celebrate the season's beauty, I try to bring the colors of fall into my home. I've found it's important to me to embrace the seasons and to feature the very best colors, imagery, sights and smells of the time.

Creating this garland of leaves is one way you could accomplish this. It can be draped atop a bookshelf or a fireplace mantel, but it is simply beautiful when strung across a window. As the sun shines through the fabric, the leaves seem to glow, mimicking the gorgeous autumn light.

MATERIALS

16-gauge dark annealed steel wire

fabric pieces

embroidery floss

1 3" × 54" (7.5cm × 137cm) fabric strip

6 1½"× 10" (4cm × 25.5cm) fabric strips

paper

pencil

TOOLS

needle-nose pliers

scissors

sewing needle

wire cutters

TECHNIQUES

Creating Wire Leaves

Creating a Fabric Garland

Sketch different leaf shapes onto a piece of paper.

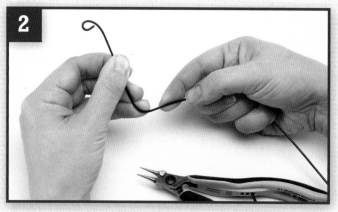

Working from the spool with 16-gauge wire, bend in the cut end flush against itself to form the tip of the stem. Bend the wire to the left at a ninety-degree angle, 3" (7.5cm) from the beginning. Gently shape your wire upward.

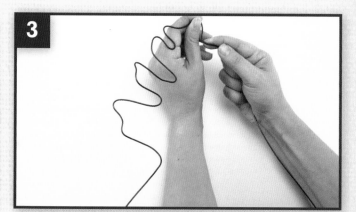

Continue to shape the wire to form the outline of a leaf. Use your sketches from Step 1 as a reference. (You can also use the template on page 125 as a guide.) When you reach the stem wire again, wrap the wire around it once.

4 Run the wire through the middle of the leaf outline to form the vein. Cut the wire, leaving excess roughly equivalent to the height of the leaf from the top tip to the end of your stem wire (about 5"–7" [13cm–18cm]). This will give you enough wire to finish the leaf.

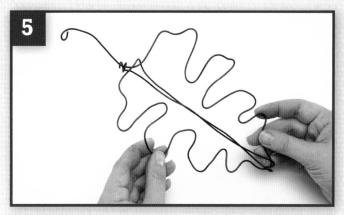

5 Run the wire back down to the stem and twist it around the stem a few times to secure it. Cut off any excess wire. You might want to give the cut end a final squeeze with your pliers after you trim the excess. Follow Steps 1–5 to create 6 leaves, varying the heights from 5"–7" (13cm–18cm).

6 Cut a 3" × 54" (7.5cm × 137cm) strip of fabric (see the tip on page 105). Cut 6 1½"× 10" (4cm × 25.5cm) small strips to hang the leaves from the large strip.

7 Choose a fabric that will let the light pass through it nicely; this project was created with a variety of batiks. Sew the fabric onto the wire leaves. Thread a small fabric strip through the small loop at the bottom of each stem. Tie each strip to the longer strip as desired.

"Autumn is a second spring when every leaf is a flower."
— ALBERT CAMUS

Quilted Christmas Ornaments

I first made these quilted ornaments the Christmas after my son was born. They were colorful and festive alternatives to ornaments that could be easily broken or potentially swallowed. I started with a basic wire ornament shape and, by adding different decorative wire embellishments to each, I was able to create an assortment of ornaments.

These can also serve as the kind of gift-package embellishments that will make your friends "oooh" and "ahh" before they even open their packages. Consider crafting some handmade ornaments next Christmas season!

MATERIALS

19-gauge craft wire

16-gauge dark annealed steel wire

embroidery floss

fabric scraps

fiberfill stuffing

wire word made from 16-gauge dark annealed steel wire: *joy* (see page 19, Steps 1 and 2)

wire flower form made from 19-gauge craft wire (see pages 15 and 16, Steps 2–5)

TOOLS

flat-nose pliers (optional)

mandrel with ¼" (6mm) or 1" (2.5cm) diameter

needle-nose pliers

scissors

sewing needle

soup can or similarly shaped object

wire cutters

TECHNIQUES

Creating a Circular or Oval-Shaped Wire Ornament

Adding Wire Elements

Using 16-gauge wire, create a loop for a bail. Wrap the wire around a soup can or similar form 2 times, returning to the top of the ornament. Wrap the wire around the base of the bail a few times and then trim any excess.

Working from the spool, pull out a 12" (30.5cm) length of 19-gauge wire. Begin wrapping the ornament with the 19-gauge wire, starting at the bottom and ending at the bail. Return to the bottom and wrap the wire from the spool up the other side of the ornament, ending at the top. Secure the wire ends by wrapping them around the bail, and then trim the excess.

"Christmas is the season for kindling the fire of hospitality in the hall, the genial flame of charity in the heart."

— WASHINGTON IRVING

To create an oval- or oblong-shaped ornament, create a round ornament as in Steps 1 and 2. Grip the top and bottom of the ornament with your hands and the form into an oval shape.

Add wire stripes to an ornament with 19-gauge wire by running the wire across the ornament, wrapping it up the side and then running it across again to the other side. Secure the wire by wrapping it back to the starting point.

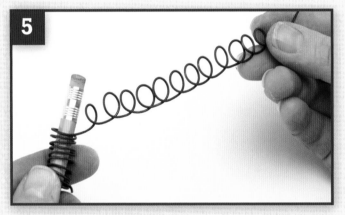

To create decorative coils, wrap 19-gauge wire around a mandrel with a ¼" (6mm) or 1" (2.5cm) diameter 15 to 20 times. Slide the coil off and press it flat to create loops. Add this border to the ornament form using the same process as for the stripes in Step 4. Add all coils or stripes before adding fabric.

Cover the ornament with scraps of fabric, wrong sides together. Stitch the fabric to the ornament, leaving a small opening for stuffing. Stuff the ornament with fiberfill, using a bamboo skewer to fill in tight spaces, and stitch the opening closed. Trim the fabric using a ¼" (6mm) allowance. Add decorative elements, such as the wire word *joy* (see page 19, Steps 1 and 2), after the fabric has been stitched. Add stitches to the wire coils or stripes.

7

To create a poinsettia for the quilted ornament, use 19-gauge wire to create a flower (see pages 15 and 16, Steps 2–5). As you shape the petals with pliers, create sharp points at the outer edges. Stitch a contrasting fabric scrap to each petal. Secure the poinsettia to the fabric portion of the ornament with a few tacking stitches.

May Day Cone

Unexpected surprises are the very best kind. In art, unexpected combinations can give us a feeling of pleased discovery. In this project, we'll play with the surprising combination of chicken wire and fabric.

Traditionally the May Day basket is filled with fresh flowers, but whether you fill your cone with cookies or a posy, it will be a wonderful surprise for the recipient. A scaled-down version of the design works great as an accent at the end of pew for a wedding, or as a chair accent for an Easter brunch. My favorite use is still as a May Day surprise, and I would love it if you were to use it to celebrate May 1 with me next spring.

MATERIALS

chicken wire

16-gauge dark annealed steel wire

¾" × 28" (71cm × 2cm) fabric strip

glue stick

spray paint (optional)

Finishing the Project

buttons

cellophane bag

fabric scraps

faux pearl necklace

ribbons

wire flower form made from 19-gauge craft wire (see pages 15 and 16, Steps 2–5)

TOOLS

needle-nose pliers

protective gloves

scissors

wire cutters

TECHNIQUES

Creating a Chicken Wire Cone

Adding Fabric to the Wire

Creating a Wire Handle

1 Using protective gloves, unroll 16" (40.5cm) of chicken wire and cut it in half lengthwise. Cut the right cut edge at a slight angle. This edge will have several sharp ends.

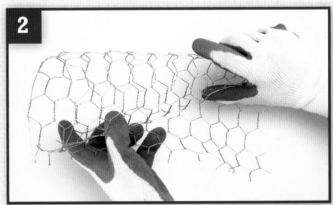

2 Roll the chicken wire into a 12" (30.5cm) long cone shape with a 4"–5" (10cm–13cm) diameter.

"The world's favorite season is the spring. All things seem possible in May."

— EDWIN WAY TEALE

Summer Sun Catcher

This sun catcher was one of my very first designs and has been a favorite in my studio for a long time. It hangs from the window year-round, and when the view is white with snow, it serves as a postcard reminding me of summer. Create one of your own, and you'll see how the light from outside flows through the fabric, brightening the entire composition.

The techniques are basic but, as always, can be developed further. What if you were to recreate an entire postcard picture of Italy in wire? What if you were to separate the different elements into multiple planes and create a shadowbox effect? A simple little sun catcher could become so much more if you take the time to let your imagination roam and play with the possibilities.

MATERIALS

19-gauge craft wire

16-gauge dark
annealed steel wire

embroidery floss

fabric pieces

fabric scraps

fabric strips

TOOLS

needle-nose pliers

scissors

sewing needle

soup can or similarly
shaped object

wire cutters

TECHNIQUES

Creating a Wire
Framework

Sewing a Patchwork
Sun with Fabric Rays

Adding Wire and
Fabric Elements

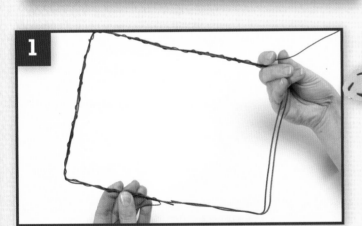

Working from the spool, create a 7" × 10" (18cm × 25.5cm)
rectangle with 16-gauge wire, wrapping the wire around twice
to create a second rectangle over the first. Holding the 2
rectangles of wire together, wrap them with 19-gauge wire.

Tip

To make each side the correct size, it's helpful
to work with a straightedge ruler placed on the
table in front of you. This way you can measure
the length of your sides and know exactly where
to make your bend.

"Rest is not idleness, and to lie sometimes on the grass under trees on a summer's
day, listening to the murmur of the water, or watching the clouds float across the
sky, is by no means a waste of time."

— JOHN LUBBOCK

Make a wire circle by wrapping 16-gauge wire around a soup can or similar circular container. Overlap the cut end by 3" (7.5cm) and cut the wire from the spool. Wrap the ends around each other once to secure. Holding the rectangle vertically, use the excess wire from the overlap in the circle to attach it to the right side of the rectangle. Use needle-nose pliers to bend in the cut ends of the wire.

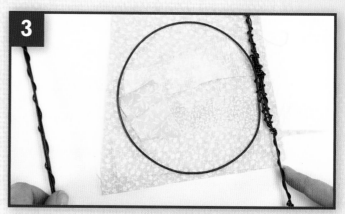

Lay out scraps of assorted yellow fabrics onto a piece of yellow fabric slightly larger than the wire sun shape, creating a patch-work effect. To check the size, it's helpful to lay the wire sun shape on top of the fabric.

Stitch the scraps to the larger piece of yellow fabric with embroidery floss.

Tie 9 ¼" (6mm) wide strips of yellow fabric to the wire sun frame, evenly spacing them around. Tie the other end of the strips to the rectangle frame as if they were rays coming out from the sun. Leave any strips that will attach to the bottom of the wire frame untied. Stitch the fabric patchwork piece to the wire sun. Trim the fabric around the sun using a ¼" (6mm) fabric allowance. Trim any excess on the rays.

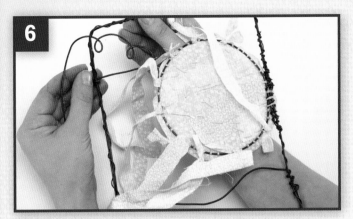

6

Form cloud shapes and the outline of a hillside from 16-gauge wire and attach them to the rectangle.

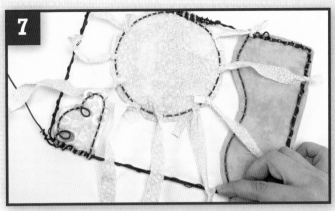

7

Hold a piece of fabric beneath the cloud and, using embroidery floss and a needle, stitch the fabric to the cloud. Trim, leaving a ¼" (6mm) allowance around the wire shape. Repeat this process to add fabric to the hillside; as you stitch, tie the rest of the fabric strips in place. To make the hanger, wrap the end of the 16-gauge wire around the top left side of the frame. Measure 9"–10" (23cm–25.5cm) and cut the wire. Bend the wire into a slight *U* shape. Wrap the other end around the top right corner of the frame. Use needle-nose pliers to bend in the cut ends of the wire.

8

Stitch a piece of blue background fabric to the rectangle, behind all the other elements. With embroidery floss, stitch a flower just above the ground piece.

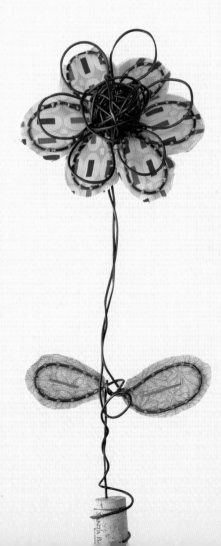

CHAPTER 8

Planning Your Growing Season

Setting Goals and Dreaming Big

Search for a gardener's calendar online and you'll most likely find a monthly guide with a timetable of garden tasks and when they should be completed. It might also tell you when to expect different plants to bloom or grow fruit. These guides are most helpful when they're regionalized because the tasks for any particular month vary according to your climate. In the upper Midwest of the United States, for example, April is the earliest we can hope to get into the garden. The tasks for this month include tilling and planting. Somewhere else in the world, April might be a time for blooms or even a harvest month. Although the timetable for the tasks might vary, essential tasks such as tilling, planting, weeding, fertilizing and harvesting are the same. We all must plant seeds before we can enjoy their bloom times as flowers. Identifying the tasks and planning for their completion is essential for the gardener.

Another planning tool many gardeners use is the journal. In it, they include sketches of what they planted each year and the location. They also record how a new crop grew and developed throughout the season, as well as changes they might make for the next year. They might keep empty seed packets in this journal for reference of what bloomed and when. With each season, this journal becomes more and more invaluable. It helps gardeners track any progress they might make toward achieving their gardening goals. If their goal is to create a perennial border that blooms continuously through the summer months, they will know from consulting their bloom records where a gap of time occurs between blooms and be able to add plants that will bloom during that gap. If their goal is a high yield in their vegetable gardens, they'll be able to mark which plants did better in a particular area of the garden and which fertilizer they applied, and in future years can adjust their garden plan accordingly.

As artists, we can use these same tools to plan and prepare for our artistic growth. Identifying our goals for our artistic gardens helps us maximize our bloom times and achieve a higher yield as we work.

Take Small Steps

To identify your goals, start with your dreams and then get specific. My "I want to be an artist" dream as a little girl could become the more specific "I want to make art my career" or "I want to make art every day." Get even more specific by asking pointed questions: What does a career in art mean to you? Do you envision yourself publishing your work or displaying it in a gallery? Or do you just want to make enough art to surround yourself with it? Although we all want to be creative and live the

inspired life, our definition of that life will vary depending on the individual. One of my friends imagines a solo show in a gallery downtown, while another wants to be able to sell enough of her art to keep her at home and out of an office. Another simply wants to make art for herself and her friends to enjoy. What dreams do you treasure? What do you want to accomplish or experience in your artistic life? What steps could you take to achieve this?

Check, check, check . . .

I'm a huge fan of to-do lists. They organize my day and prioritize my tasks. My daily to-do lists usually start with two or three things I've already done, just so I have something to cross off right away. This gets a little tricky at the start of the day, but I have no shame and will write *get out of bed, make coffee* and *write to-do list* if I don't have anything else to start my list. My husband mocks me terribly for this, but it motivates me and makes me feel as though my day is off to a positive start.

I also have great big dreamy to-do lists with items like *travel the world, attend an art retreat in Italy, teach at an art retreat in Italy* and *paint sunflowers in Provence*. I make lists for my art, too. The one I have hanging in my studio has items like *make a big wire star with lights* and *learn to silkscreen*. These are things I'd like to do someday when I have the time. When those rare moments of free time finally come and I'm able to play, I have a list of to-dos ready and waiting.

In the last few years, I've learned it's not enough to just dream. I need to commit to a goal, think out the steps to actualize it and plan the resources and time to accomplish it. This takes self-discipline, which was something I didn't think I had until my husband and I

decided to take control of our finances. We made goals, planned how we would reach them and then continually motivated ourselves. When we did this, I saw what was possible and began to apply those same principles of goal planning to other areas in my life. That's when I first decided to submit my work to magazines and when my Etsy store came into being. I realized if I wanted to make my goals a reality, I had to take action. It was great to make to-do lists, but I needed to actually follow them and not just dream about them. The process starts with dreaming, but it can't end there. To make our dreams real, we need to take a step toward them. Start with a little step. Turn off the television and focus on your art one night a week. Go to the library and browse the art section, find something you want to learn and do it! Join an online knitting community and commit to a row a day. Sign up for the monoprint workshop you've thought of trying or a memoir writing class. It doesn't matter how little your first step; the point is that it's a first step. After that, commit yourself to taking the next step and the next, continuing as far as you can until you can't take another. Like the mountain climber, you might find you can't go any farther because you've reached the pinnacle. There aren't any remaining steps, so you must go down and find yourself a new mountain to climb.

Use your sketchbook and journal to dream in and to plan as you go. Make them a reference so that when your next winter comes, you can use the time to plan intelligently for your next spring. Perhaps the monoprint workshop led to some ideas for creating your own printed cloth. Write those ideas down! Later, when you have the time or resources available, you'll be able to pursue those ideas. If

Cultivating Inspiration

Create a Gardener's Journal for Your Life

Do a little research into gardeners' planning journals and then create one of your own. It can include photos of your "growing moments" as well as notes on what you learned. You can create pockets to hold objects, seed packets or anything else you picked up on your journey. Be sure to make suggestions for next year's garden and write about what worked and didn't work this year. Make a map of your artistic garden, specifying all the creative interests you have. Do you quilt, cook and decorate? Create an area for each, plus a couple blank areas for you to experiment with something new. Make a monthly, weekly or yearly guide of tasks or steps you plan to take so you can grow. Then celebrate your bloom time. Take photos and make notes on how you feel as you achieve your goals; this section will be your motivation during next year's planning and preparation time. Continue to cultivate your garden and keep this journal, and plan for years of growth and beauty in your artistic life.

your coffee meeting with other local artists resulted in some information about local craft fairs that are particularly suited for your art, make a note of them, even if you don't plan to exhibit in the near future. You're gathering ideas and information that will benefit you at another stage of your journey.

Dry spells will come, and there will be winters that never seem to end, but by preparing and planning for those times you can weather them successfully. You can plant knowledgeably and with foresight. You can amend your soil by thinking like a designer and force yourself to grow by challenging yourself. By making use of your tools, you can plant and harvest a bountiful artistic life. Cultivate inspiration in your life and let your life be an encouragement for others to do the same. Be the artist you want to be. Love your life and let it bloom, starting today.

Scribble Heart Studio Talisman

It's surprising to me how strong a connection I feel toward certain images. One that I use repeatedly in my work is the heart. It's a symbol important to so many people, speaking to them of love or passion. It can represent kindness or compassion, or it can speak to you of your dreams and aspirations.

My scribble heart with wings represents my artist's soul, free and able to fly. It can soar into the clouds or skim the edge of the ocean, wherever my dreams lead it. I think of it as my talisman. It hangs in my studio, and as I work it reminds me I am allowing my heart to fly free through my art.

You can personalize your scribble heart by including symbols, fabrics, quotes or anything else you feel describes who you are. Make your heart meaningful to you. Then hang it in your home as a visible and potent representation of your artist's heart.

MATERIALS

- buttons
- 19-gauge craft wire
- 16-gauge dark annealed steel wire
- embroidery floss
- fabric strips
- found objects
- glue stick
- old paintbrush
- paper strips

TOOLS

- needle-nose pliers
- scissors
- wire cutters

TECHNIQUES

Creating a Wire Scribble Heart

Adding Fabric to the Scribble Heart

Personalizing the Scribble Heart

Notes on the Process

The first scribble heart I made was tossed into the corner where I keep all my mistakes. I'd been aiming for something a little airier and less "scribbly," and I felt I'd gotten carried away with wrapping and weaving the wire. A day or two went by, and the project kept coming to mind, so I picked it up out of the mistake pile and took another look. I decided to hang it up in the bedroom. After a month my husband and I decided the heart had grown on us. It's now one of my all-time favorite designs. It's a "mistake" that proved a keeper. Now I try not to judge my work by how it compares to what I had in mind, but to see if it has merit of its own, just like my scribble heart.

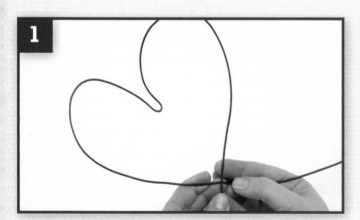

1 Working from the spool, form a large heart shape from 16-gauge wire, starting and ending at the bottom of the heart. Cut the wire, leaving a small amount of excess.

2 To keep the shape of your heart, secure it at the bottom by twisting the cut ends together with needle-nose pliers. Bend them under to secure.

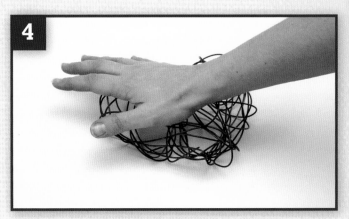

Working from the spool, loosely wrap and weave the wire around the heart shape until it starts to take on a 3-D form. Cut the wire, leaving 12" (30.5cm) excess to weave through the heart. Feel free to wrap and weave as much as you want.

I think the scribble heart looks better when it's a little squished. Set the heart on a hard surface and push against it with the palm of your hand to flatten it slightly.

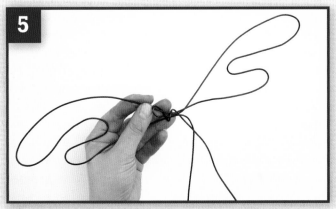

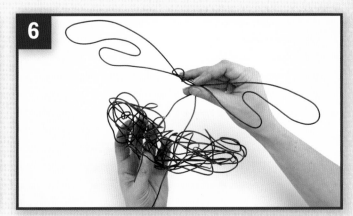

Form a pair of wings from 16-gauge wire by forming 1 wing, wrapping the wire at the center and then forming the second wing. Cut the wire from the spool, leaving some excess for fastening it to the heart.

Insert the excess wire from the wings through the scribbles on the back of the heart, bending the wire to secure. If the wings aren't securely attached, use 19-gauge wire to attach the elements more snugly.

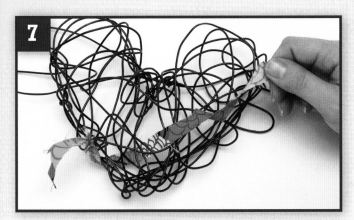

7

Tie 1 end of a fabric strip to a wire on the heart. Thread the rest of the strip through and around the heart. Tie the other end to another scribble to secure. Repeat this process as often as desired. Be sure to weave strips through the wire, as this creates depth.

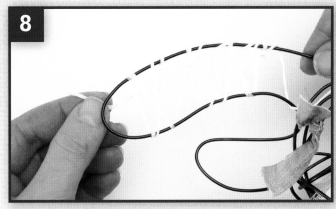

8

Tie 1 end of a skein of embroidery floss near the base of your wings. Wrap the floss once around the top wire, and then bring it down to the bottom wire. Wrap the bottom wire twice and then bring it up to the top wire again. Repeat this process, moving across the entire length of the wing. Once you've wrapped half the wing, start to wrap a little more haphazardly. Continue until the entire wing has been wrapped. Repeat this step with the second wing.

9

Choose objects and sayings to include in the heart to personalize it and give it meaning. Include tools of your trade (like an old paintbrush), buttons or pretty found objects you've collected. Attach these items with 1"–2" (2.5cm–5cm) pieces of 19-gauge wire bent into *U* shapes, or simply insert them through the scribbles (as was the case with my paintbrush). Weave strips of paper with inspirational quotes or your favorite sayings through the wire, or wrap 1 end around a wire and use a glue stick to secure it.

Resolutions Wall Quilt

It's become part of our culture's common parlance to speak of goals when we speak of success. We must dream up goals, write them down and use them to envision what we want. Don't you hear those admonitions all the time? I always did, and, really, it got somewhat annoying. In fact, it just made me feel guilty for not complying.

In the last couple years, however, I discovered what an impact goals could make in my life. It makes a difference to set short-, medium- and long-term goals. It feels good to achieve my short-term goals and make significant steps toward my long-term goals as well. Now I love to write down my goals.

This is a good project to try if you're ready to set and achieve some goals. It's also an ideal way to become familiar with art-quilting techniques. If trying something new is one of your goals, creating this project will allow you to cross it off your list. Talk about motivation!

MATERIALS

- adhesive-backed hook-and-loop tape
- 16-gauge dark annealed steel wire
- embroidery floss
- fabric scraps
- fusible interfacing
- glue stick
- inkjet printable paper-backed fabric
- quilt backing fabric
- quilt batting
- quilt top fabric
- Ranger Distress Ink
- 14" (35.5cm) tree branch
- wire clothes hanger

wire word made from 19-gauge craft wire: *growth* (see page 19, Steps 1 and 2)

Finishing the Project
- beads
- buttons
- fringe or rickrack trim
- pearls
- ribbons

TOOLS

- ink applicator
- inkjet printer
- iron
- ironing board
- needle-nose pliers
- scissors
- sewing needle

spray bottle with water

wire cutters

TECHNIQUES

Creating a Fabric Panel

Distressing Photo Fabric and Adding Text

Creating Removable Resolutions

Hanging the Wall Quilt

Layer a 18½" × 25" (47cm × 63.5cm) piece of quilt top fabric over a 17½" × 24" (44.5cm × 61cm) piece of quilt batting and stitch them together with embroidery floss and a running stitch.

Using an inkjet printer, print a list of resolutions and a title onto paper-backed fabric. Cut the resolutions and title text apart with scissors, separating each phrase into several sections. With an ink applicator, rub Distress Ink onto the edges of the text pieces. Spritz water onto the inked areas right away to give the text pieces a distressed look. Remove the paper backing.

"People who are unable to motivate themselves must be content with mediocrity, no matter how impressive their other talents."

— ANDREW CARNEGIE

Templates

Bird 1
Two Birds on a Branch, page 70

Bird 2
Birdhouse Assemblage, page 48
Two Birds on a Branch, page 70
For the *Birdhouse Assemblage* project,
make a bird with only one wing.

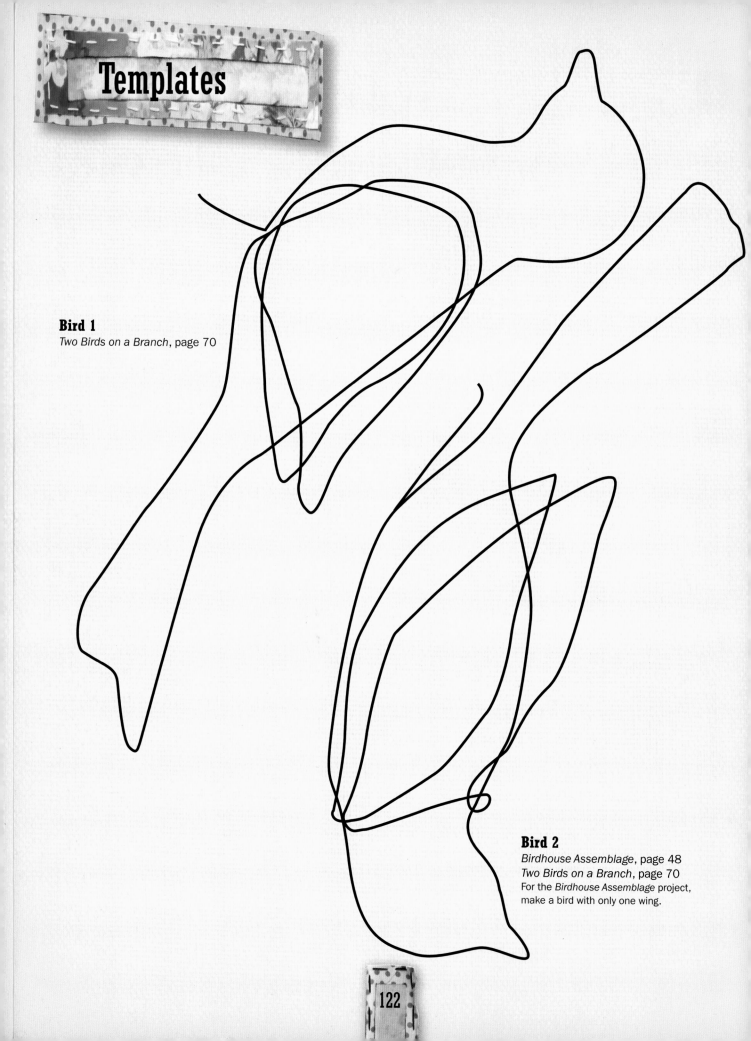

Large Butterfly
Butterfly Flight Table Lamp, page 66

Wire Word *home*
Birdhouse Assemblage, page 48

Small Butterfly
Butterfly Flight Table Lamp, page 66

Wire Word *coffee*
*Coffee Conversational
Photo Holder, page 37*

Wire Word *artist*
Artist's Badge, page 18

Wire Words *create,* *dream* and *inspired*

Inspiration Board, page 30
Altered Canvas Bag, page 54
For the *Inspiration Board*, omit the letter *d* in *inspired*.

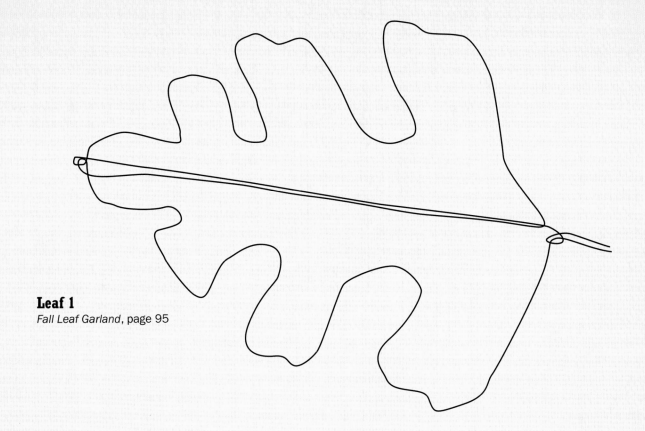

Leaf 1
Fall Leaf Garland, page 95

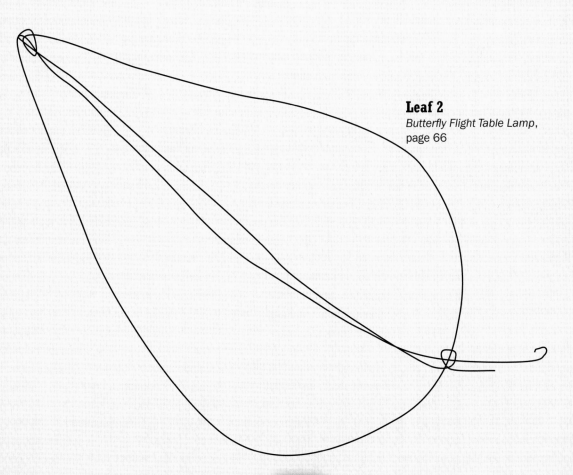

Leaf 2
Butterfly Flight Table Lamp,
page 66

Resources

Wire

Darice
www.darice.com
*small rolls of 19-gauge craft wire;
can usually be found at your local
craft store*

Grip-Rite
www.grip-rite.com
*3½ lb. spools of 16-gauge tie wire;
can usually be found at your local
hardware store in the rebar section*

Fabric

Alexander Henry Fabrics
www.ahfabrics.com

Hoffman Fabrics
www.hoffmanfabrics.com

In the Beginning Fabrics
www.inthebeginningfabrics.com

Joel Dewberry
www.joeldewberry.com

Moda Fabrics
www.modafabrics.com

Mixed-Media Supplies

Derwent
www.pencils.co.uk
*Inktense pencils and other mark-
making supplies*

Golden Artist Colors
www.goldenpaints.com
acrylic paints and mediums

ICE Resin
www.iceresin.com
nontoxic jeweler's-grade resin

Oxford Impressions
www.oxfordimpressions.com
photo-realistic art stamps

Polyform Products Company
www.sculpey.com
*Studio by Sculpey oven-bake
polymer clay*

Ranger Ink
www.rangerink.com
*mixed-media products and
supplies, including the craft sheet*

Single Stone Studios
www.singlestonestudios.com
art stamps

Miscellaneous

IKEA
www.ikea.com
*basic furniture and lighting
to embellish*

Otto Frei
www.ottofrei.com
jewelry tools

Online Sources for Inspiration

1000 Markets
www.1000markets.com
handmade goods

DaWanda
www.dawanda.com
handmade goods

Etsy
www.etsy.com
handmade goods

Flickr
www.flickr.com
photo-sharing site

Indie Craft Shows
www.indiecraftshows.com
find craft shows in your area

Index

Nurture your creativity with North Light Books!

Bent, Bound & Stitched
Collage, Cards and Jewelry
with a Twist
Giuseppina Cirincione

Bent, Bound & Stitched features beautiful step-by-step collage projects, as well as a variety of mixed-media techniques. Learn how to bend and shape wire into letters and numbers, use a sewing wheel and acrylic paint to add texture to papers, make hinges from a portion of a rubber stamp, combine different gauges of wire to create different looks and rework found objects into jewelry. *Bent, Bound & Stitched* is one piece of eye candy you will want to pull off your shelf again and again.

paperback, 128 pages
ISBN-10: 1-60061-060-9
ISBN-13: 978-1-60061-060-8
Z1752

Creative Time & Space
Making Room for Making Art
Ricë Freeman-Zachery

Discover secrets for keeping the creative part of your brain engaged throughout the day and pull yourself out of a creative rut with ideas from an insider's look into the studios of several successful artists. In her inspiring follow-up to *Living the Creative Life*, author Ricë Freeman-Zachery has gathered together a new band of artists to share their time-finding tricks and studio-savvy tips to help you find your own *Creative Time & Space*.

paperback with flaps, 144 pages
ISBN-10: 1-60061-322-5
ISBN-13: 978-1-60061-322-7
Z2953

Taking Flight
Inspiration & Techniques to Give Your Creative Spirit Wings
Kelly Rae Roberts

In *Taking Flight*, you'll find inspiration to grow your creative wings. Learn the mixed-media painting techniques Kelly Rae Roberts employs to create her artwork, including layering paints and incorporating meaningful phrases. Follow prompts to begin your own creative journey—look for the sacred in the ordinary and embrace your fears, then incorporate what you find into your art. Take further inspiration from gallery projects by the author and contributors. Spread your artistic wings and make art of your own!

paperback, 128 pages
ISBN-10: 1-60061-082-X
ISBN-13: 978-1-60061-082-0
Z1930

These and other fine North Light titles are available at your local craft retailer, bookstore or online supplier, or visit our website at www.mycraftivitystore.com.